FREEDOM AT WORK
LANGUAGE, PROFESSIONAL, AND INTELLECTUAL DEVELOPMENT IN SCHOOLS

MARÍA E. TORRES-GUZMÁN

WITH RUTH SWINNEY

Paradigm Publishers
Boulder • London

Copyright © 2010 Paradigm Publishers

Published in the United States by Paradigm Publishers, 3360 Mitchell Lane, Suite E, Boulder, CO 80301 USA.

Paradigm Publishers is the trade name of Birkenkamp & Company, LLC, Dean Birkenkamp, President and Publisher.

Library of Congress Cataloging-in-Publication Data

Torres-Guzmán, María E.
  Freedom at work : language, professional, and intellectual development in schools / María E. Torres-Guzmán with Ruth Swinney.
      p. cm. — (Series in critical narrative)
  Includes bibliographical references and index.
  ISBN 978-1-59451-699-3 (hardcover : alk. paper)
  ISBN 978-1-59451-700-6 (paperback : alk. paper)
  1. Teachers—In-service training—United States. 2. Teacher-principal relationships—United States. 3. Language and education—United States. 4. Multiculturalism—United States. I. Swinney, Ruth. II. Title. III. Title: Language,
professional, and intellectual development in schools. IV. Series.
  LB1731.T63 2009
  370.71'55—dc22
                                                                                        2009002631

Printed and bound in the United States of America on acid-free paper that meets the standards of the American National Standard for Permanence of Paper for Printed Library Materials.

Designed and Typeset by Straight Creek Bookmakers.

13 12 11 10   2 3 4 5

FREEDOM AT WORK

Series in Critical Narrative
Edited by Donaldo Macedo
University of Massachusetts–Boston

In memory of my father,
Santos Torres-Colon

CONTENTS

ACKNOWLEDGMENTS

This book has been in the making for many years; there are many to whom I have a debt of gratitude.

Mil gracias to Ruth Swinney, for the many years of conversations and for her courage, her inspirational story, and her friendship. Ruth's creative work is center to this book, and my hope is that through it and through her work she will continue to be a shining light.

To all the PS 165 teachers I have collaborated with and from whom I have gained insights about schooling. For the children and the parents who have permitted me to observe, interview, and videotape in the classrooms over the years. Special thanks go to Davekin Ynoa for his drawing of the school.

To my dear friends, Ursula Casanova, Bertha Perez, Javier King, Feli Etxeberria, and Paquita Orbe for their encouragement and, in some cases, multiple readings. Every time you asked me when the book would come out, I heard your urgency and assurance that I had something to say. To two very special colleagues, Eduardo Hernandez-Chavez and Maxine Greene, your critiques helped me think through many of my ideas.

To my graduate students who got involved over the years, helping me do the research—gathering data, doing library searches, transcribing, coding, and the like—many, many thanks.

To members of my family who have heard the stories a million times and are patient enough to listen one more time. Three members, in particular, have been supporting me with all types of care—my mother, Catalina Guzman; my daughter, Nydia Zamorano-Torres; and my husband, Juan Olivas. Juan's challenging comments always went to the heart of my doubts, and I emerged stronger in my beliefs as a result. *Muchisimas gracias.*

My gratitude also goes out to Donaldo Macedo, the series editor, who believed in me, and the editorial staff, who made the book a reality.

I

*ENMARCANDO/*AN INTRODUCTION

This book is about freedom in education. Freedom is defined within as a state of being as well as a social measure of how we are living our lives. Freedom is defined very concretely within a particular place and at a given time. This, in part, is a reaction to the talk about freedom that is never defined. We think about freedom as important to how well we are doing. However, when we measure how well we are doing, we tend to look at the individual's or group's income or at the GNP of a nation. Amartya Sen, a Nobel Prize–winning economist, proposes that we stop and think about what we mean when we say we are living well. He proposes that instead of income or GNP we use the concept of freedom as a measure of development.[1] Since freedom is so vital a human desire, Sen proposes we may get further in understanding our existence in this world by actually measuring freedoms instead of money. There is a basic freedom that he calls substantive freedom, which roughly speaking is what Roosevelt called the freedom from want—the freedom to be able to get basic human needs such as food and shelter. Instrumental freedoms are associated with social opportunities, such as education, health care, employment, voting and political campaigning, and the like. Sen proposes that to guarantee what an individual wants and values, freedom needs to exist in the institutional structures, in our cultural ethos, in the human relationships we establish. Freedom is a social construction and, thus, to guarantee individual freedoms we have to create social freedoms that support them. Therefore, there is an essential relationship between individual and social freedoms.

Sen goes further. He proposes that freedom cannot be seen just as a process but needs to come into existence as an outcome as well. Freedoms, whichever they may be, must result in the expansion of freedoms. In other words, as we individually step into our freedoms, we have a responsibility to bring along others with us so that as a community we can sustain the way of life we want. Expanding those freedoms is development.

In today's world, however, many of the freedoms we have enjoyed are under siege. Some of the freedoms that teachers enjoyed in the past have been thwarted in the name of standardization and accountability. My experience with a New York City administrator and a teachers group working to transform a school brought me to question the effects these movements have on limiting freedoms in schools.

What I learned as the school ethnographer was that it was precisely in the freedoms the principal afforded the teachers within the school, and into which individual teachers stepped to take ownership of their own professional development, that the enthusiasm for creating a better educational world for the children rested. Looking back at the ease with which I observed teachers entering the principal's office to have a conversation with me or with the principal about what they had experienced in the classroom, to share a display of what the children had accomplished, or to get our opinion about something they were thinking about doing is not an everyday sight in many schools, especially schools with large populations of diverse language and cultural minorities living in poverty and in the inner city. On the contrary, what we tend to see in the high-poverty and minority schools are closer scrutiny and more rigid controls.

The story within, of Public School 165[2] in the Manhattan Valley of New York City, challenges the effectiveness of the forms of scrutiny and controls we are required to follow within our low-resourced and low-performing schools. Within, I will provide the evidence for my assertions.

Rather than focus on the standardization of school curricula, that is, on making what we provide children in schools uniform and conforming to what is measured on tests, the work at PS 165 taught me that we ought to spend more time and effort in assisting children in understanding the knowledge we already have and in helping them make it their own. Furthermore, rather than focus on the sum of test scores as the measure of accountability of the teacher, we need to speak about the adult world's sense of social responsibility and how it might appear in the individual and social worlds our young experience.[3]

The point is, we can talk about standardization and accountability as a way of achieving equity but we have ample evidence that the freedoms within the curriculum, what is taught and what is measured, are curtailed, and the outcomes are greater gaps.

Within, I highlight how a leader's resolve on language equity and her moral imperative of social justice—that not only included the culturally and linguistically diverse populations, but that made them the center of all the school's work—injected a school with new possibilities even when it was under the threat of closure. The ease with which the teachers and I entered Principal Ruth Swinney's office was reflective of our trust of each other, and this trust was based on a shared understanding of our social responsibility with respect to the children and their communities. Our social responsibility and trust in each other created an atmosphere that did not hold up the traditional boundaries that individual roles and status called for. The boundaries were blurred and/or made seamless in the spirit of our goal—to turn around an environment of miseducation[4] to one where the very same children could thrive. The tasks were not easy, as the school was in disarray physically, emotionally, and intellectually. The state's threat to close the school was looming over it when Ruth arrived at its door as principal. Yet, six years later, when she retired, those of us that stayed could say that the school had survived, persisted, and flourished to the point of being acknowledged for what was going on in its instructional and administrative arenas.[5]

When I thought about what was accomplished and the legacy Ruth left, I could see that what occurred could be identified as emerging from one kind of development—professional development, as it was organized as a freedom. It was organized as such because the school was faced with the task of developing the teachers' capabilities to work with the culturally and linguistically diverse student population. It would have been efficient to organize staff development in traditional ways, but there were issues of theory development and appropriateness of application, of having sufficient staff developers with the specific expertise needed, and of having sufficient funding in an atmosphere of decreasing budgets that made alternative structures necessary. The more powerfully democratic route was to encourage the teachers to take on the ownership and responsibility for their own and their colleagues' development.

3

The path was based on a deep understanding of (and faith in) human beings and their motivations. It was also based on an understanding that creativity, which is what this complex educational situation called for, required a level of freedom to engage in professional work. The work of bilingualism was at a new stage; we were then experimenting with different components—the organization of the school, the philosophy toward an underprivileged group, the use of multiple languages, the development of teachers, etc. The outcome of the school personnel's work would be the result of much more than technocratic complacency. It was not sufficient to learn new methods, the process of transformation in the school required passion, enthusiasm, and creativity. The entire school community would reap the benefits of having a teacher community that was excited about its work. The teachers felt they were in the driver's seat every day because they were valued and treated as truly worthy of wearing the badge of teachers. It was the ethos of professional development as freedom that gave room to the developments that took place in the school—those that I could later describe as language and intellectual freedoms. Freedom was, thus, generating even more freedom and the freedoms were in two areas key to education—language and intellectual development.

It was in this context that I worked with individual teachers like Loraine Lagos, Peter Richardson, Victoria Hunt, Belinda Arana, Amanda Hartman, Berta Alvarez, Estrella Magnam, Isabel Fletcha, Peter Kenzer, Rebecca Madrigal, Estrella Magallan, Rachel Bard, Aida Cajas (later Genovese) and many more.[6] Some of them were my former students; quite a few were not. They were each individually committed to the education of bilingual learners,[7] language equity, and social justice. They individually and collectively contributed to this book by what they did daily in their classrooms, by what we did together during the slivers of time we met during the school day, before and after the children's presence was felt at the school, and by what we did on Saturdays and during the summers.

As individuals and in groups, they taught me what thinking deeply about the education of bilingual learners means; how to think about the linguistic freedoms that are necessary for full intellectual development; and how to sit down with colleagues in total freedom to speak about their wants, desires, accomplishments, and failures. My work with them contributed to my own professional and intellectual development. I propose that the needs of bilingual learners need to be placed in a conversation of freedom because their intellectual developmental processes call for learning to be at its fullest, and to do this the teachers need to have the freedom to access all the resources (linguistic, social, and cognitive) at their disposal.[8] Anything less will not provide them with an optimal learning environment. The intellectual and the linguistic go hand in hand. We construct much of our thought, beliefs, and values through and with language. Thus, we must take all the linguistic resources into account when we think of developing students cognitively and socially. In this context, my own desires were satiated and wanting at the same time. I enjoyed my work in the school context but I had to think of ways of extending freedom in other domains of my life. I needed to create an extended professional community in my own work place at the College and in academia while extending academia to the schools. In spite of the fact that I was a faculty member at Teachers College, the work of the college and my work in the schools seemed to be miles apart. At the school, I was always engaged in trying to understand and connect with prevailing theories, particularly those theories promoting reflective practices and collaboration with schools. At the College, I was always testing new ideas I read and heard about in the context of the lived experiences at the schools with which I worked. There were times when I believed the twain would never meet, although I always felt that what I was experiencing was the classical case of disconnect between theory and practice: I just did not know how to bridge it and bring my colleagues into the conversation. The book before you is one of the ways I felt I could begin to bring some of the tensions of theory and practice into the academic world in which I also live.

FROM GRAY TO COLOR: THE WHY OF THE STUDY

Six years had passed since I first went to the school. I remember the day Ruth invited me to Public School 165. Ring, ring! It was early September when Ruth called. PS 165 was about ten blocks away; we made the appointment. Upon climbing the stairs and going through the institutional gray doors at the school, I found barren walls and desolate hallways. The walls in the classrooms did not have much life yet. Around the corner, I found the principal's office. Ruth Swinney was waiting for me. She stood up and we began walking down the hall. "I call this the Savage Inequality Tour,"[9] she said. I would soon learn why.

We went up stairways with electric cables hanging from the ceilings, the tiles on the floor of the first floor were missing, and the auditorium was in shambles. The building was a 100-year-old elegantly designed

5

structure by Charles B. J. Snyder[10] that was in a complete state of decay. Since her appointment as principal at PS 165, just a month or so before school began, the then New York City Board of Education was facing the biggest asbestos clean up in its history. I had read about the asbestos problem in the *New York Times*. One of the articles mentioned not just the asbestos problem but also the roof leaks and other symptoms of long-term neglect of the buildings.[11] Ruth had almost immediately gone public, as asbestos was only one of the school building's concerns. In addition, there were roof leaks and many, many maintenance problems.

"I had just enough time to put the furniture back into the classrooms once the asbestos was removed," she told me. The water leaks, peeling paint, dangerous stairways, and loose wiring were still a common sight when the children walked in the door that fall. Abandonment and lack of commitment to the upkeep and maintenance of the physical plant were the best descriptors of the state of affairs at the school. Beautification of the physical plant meant that Ruth had to deal with the closed circles of the city's janitorial staff. "Oh, did she have work ahead of her," I thought. It reminded me of Freire's questions when he first visited the Sao Pablo schools.[12] "Why does [the educational] rhetoric not include hygiene, cleanliness, [and] beauty? Why does it neglect the indisputable pedagogical value of the 'materiality' of the school environment?"

Ugliness, unhappiness, and hopelessness were not just present in the physical plant; they were the essence of the intellectual fabric of the school. Ruth told me that the academic performance of the children was amongst the poorest in the city. Only 17 percent of children at the school were reading on grade level. The challenges were many. The school had a 97 percent poverty level amongst its student population, 60 percent was non-English speaking, and their mobility rate was 33 percent. "It is a SURR[13] school," she said. Listed as a school under review by the state meant that the school was in danger of being dismantled as a district school and reopened directly under state control. The school district had been slowly giving in to the dismantling of the school by placing two growing alternative schools in the building. This was Ruth's reference in naming the tour after Kozol's legendary book, *Savage Inequality*. She wanted each visitor—city mover and shaker or educator—that went through this tour to be disturbed by what was seen and imagined.

The contrast was on the third floor. Upon entering this doorway, a flush of color gave way to a different reality in the school's alternative elementary school. Walking in, the new children-size furniture on this floor was a stark contrast. The stimulating, bright colored rugs on the floor and displays of children's work appeared almost immediately upon starting school. A furtive look inside of the alternative schools' classrooms gave the visitor a sense of quality academic environments where boys and girls, as individuals and in groups, engaged, and were engaging others, in learning activities. Within the same building, mostly white, middle-class, ivy-league families (from the Columbia University and Bank Street College neighborhoods close by) had a haven for the respectful treatment of their children as learners.

On the fifth floor was a small alternative middle school also catering to the middle-class population in the surrounding area.

PS 165, in contrast, was a school in crisis—sandwiched in juxtaposition to two fairly model-like middle-class, mainstream schools—requiring new organizational structures, new ways of knowing about teaching, and new strategies for teacher development and for improving the education students received. The starkness of the contrast and the potentially dark future of PS 165 filled me with sadness and discomfort. It was Ruth's intention to make visible the unfairness of this disparity to those who wanted to open their hearts to see.

PS 165 is located on the Upper West Side of New York City, on the southern borders of Columbia University and three streets from Bank Street College. The row of brownstones on the north side of the street was shabby looking with graffiti on the walls. There were 11 shelters for the homeless around the school. The street was grimy and full of trash. In September 1993 the neighborhood was a tough, crime- and drug-infested area with a significant amount of gang activity.[14] Scaffolds around the school building gave the drug dealers an opportunity to hide crack vials. As we visited the playground, Ruth picked one up. She told me the vials could be found all around the school grounds. One morning, after a weekend, she had picked up more than 80 vials. All the complaints to the School Construction Authority went unheard. She would soon make the condition of the neighborhood known to friends and foes alike. She made the local interdenominational church, Riverside Church, and the police precinct her allies. At one point, full of rage, Ruth dumped a big bag of crack vials on the School Construction Authority's top officer's desk, asking him, "Would you want your kids to be confronted by that? If it is not good enough for your kids; it is not good enough for anybody else's kids." Ruth expressed her rage because she believed that allowing the children to step over crack vials every day on their way to school could be avoided. She believed that this would never have been allowed in one of the downtown schools in the district, while in this poor, immigrant community it was allowed to occur with everybody's knowledge and understanding. After the confrontation with the head of the School Construction Authority, things began to change.

It was Ruth's belief that this kind of confrontation was necessary to publicly acknowledge that the children of immigrants did not count as much as other children. There were many ways in which she saw this differential treatment occurring. In the alternative schools, the children enjoyed nice furniture and sufficient supplies of materials, while PS 165 children did not. The PS 165 lunchroom was full of personnel that had been dismissed from other schools, including a worker who could be found shooting drugs in the bathroom during lunchtime. Poor immigrant children just counted less. Ruth would rhetorically ask, "Who are the children that count and how does the society, in this case, the district, show the different ways of caring for kids according to social status?"

The neighbors were watching. The new principal would disturb and threaten some of the neighbors' way of life. They nicknamed Ruth the "white bitch." In the lunchroom, she found some parents feeding their fifth-grade children; some waited for their children outside the classroom door. She told these parents to leave her school if all they did was waste their time and not give their children the support they needed to develop socially. By the second month, some of the parents were picketing to boot her out. Death threats were part of her reality. At a holiday gathering, upon arrival, Ruth and a couple of teachers talked about a neighborhood woman who had just threatened Ruth. She described a vivid, yet horrific image. The woman told her, "You need to be careful. If not, you can look forward to leaving horizontally."

Ruth had consciously stepped into this school. She had told me once, "I want a very big challenge because if I cannot turn around a failing school, all my rhetoric is not worth much." She knew that this school was in a poor, primarily Latino community. As in many other schools in our nation's inner cities, the students were abandoned to physical mayhem, intellectual famine, and linguistic chaos. These children did not have all the basic, substantive, and instrumental freedoms[15] that were embodied in the white middle-class existence nor in the expectations and norms governing our nation's public schools. The children of the neighborhood faced the many unfreedoms of poverty. A good number of the students were the children of street-corner vendors of flowers; they lived in basement cubicles infested with rats almost the size of cats; a few of the children came in with rat bites. They faced a life of unfreedoms as they could not afford basic needs, such as safe places to live in or healthy food to eat. Many parents were not gainfully employed. The unfreedoms were economic and social. Many parents were also from minoritized language[16] groups facing the unfreedoms of voicing who they were or what they desired in the English-speaking world that governed their surroundings.

People's expectations are structured as freedoms and restraints as well. An example of how this occurred was with Midori's[17] visit to PS 165. When a donor asked Ruth what she needed in the school, she responded that the school needed a music program for the children. After the gift of a baby grand piano there was a connection made with New York City's philharmonic school program; then came a visit by the violinist Midori. Midori had a New York City community initiative that focused on access to classical music for children of all walks of life. PS 165 became one of these access points. When the school district found out that Midori had been invited to the school, one of the central district personnel suggested to Ruth that it would be a waste if the event were not opened to other parents, as the parents of PS 165 would not know how to appreciate her talents. Ruth was furious when she heard this and decided to close the event to her school parents exclusively. She, and her staff, believed that if they did not have high expectations, no programs would be set up to give the children opportunities to be exposed and, thus, created unfreedoms—in this case the restricting of opportunities for children to be their best.

In the United States, educational institutions are far from equipped to truly free the children of the poor, minority, non-English speaking communities to learn, to think, to imagine, and to act according to our societies' expectations. Ruth, however, refused to accept the "inferior" positioning of the minoritized language child as fair.[18] Her first day in the school she had to carry in her own boxes of material, as the janitorial staff would not even offer to assist her. In her office, she found the furniture to consist of a broken-down table and an old desk. All she could think of while walking through the "bloody mess," as Ruth put it, was that what she found was not accidental. The leaking roof, the asbestos, the broken desks, the hanging wires were all indicative of how schools valued the kids and their communities. She was very angry. She had worked in the top schools in the district, and they were not in these same conditions. Why the differential treatment? It was clear to her that the condescending attitude of the district allowed the school to be "horrible," year after year. The school building was allowed to get this way. All she could do was compare. She threatened to bring in the newspapers to come take pictures of the conditions of her and the alternative schools' spaces. Visually they were worlds apart, although they were in the same building. When I asked her what made her roll up her sleeves rather than throw in the towel, she told me that she was pragmatic and always felt that, confronted with a problem, the next step was to see how to fix or solve it. She had set herself up for the challenge and she was committed to build the school's capabilities in addressing the issues children in this community faced. She was willing to stand for redefining education for minoritized language children; she was willing to "redefine bilingualism and cultural pluralism as positive qualities."[19] Thus, she started her tenure by taking the school district chancellor, board members, and anyone who would visit her school through the tour of savage inequalities.

That was then, six years ago. On my first visit to the school after Ruth's retirement, I consciously tried to recall my first day in the school. I wanted to recall the then and now to compare, to see what was different. At the top of the first set of stairs, I saw the first piece of evidence of Ruth's legacy; it triggered in me the memories of the transformation I had witnessed over the years. The gray doors that had marked the entrance to the administration floor were now bursting with color. The school's physical appearance had changed significantly. As we later talked about what happened, Ruth reminded me, "I had to initiate a chocolate sale to buy the paint." Teachers collaborated with the studio in a school arts program, also housed within the school building, to transform the door with imprints of scenes and feelings experienced in PS 165. Teachers raised thousands of dollars to assist the school in a variety of projects. And, in Ruth's second year, she started engaging a few benefactors in an effort to reconstruct the physical plant, as this became one of her initial priorities. By the end of the six years, there were many donations. Between donations and teacher fundraising, Ruth left behind the baby grand piano; a reconstructed building; and the legacy of a vibrant, colorful, and beautifully designed playground like those found in many middle-class schools.

Children-sized sofas and chairs appeared in the hallways and corners, bought with chocolate money. Money from chocolate sales, led by Ruth, went to the school's petty cash fund that financed many extras for the children of this low-resourced school; they did not have the luxury of having parents with the resources and know-how to raise funds for the

Figure 1.1: PS 165 Timeline

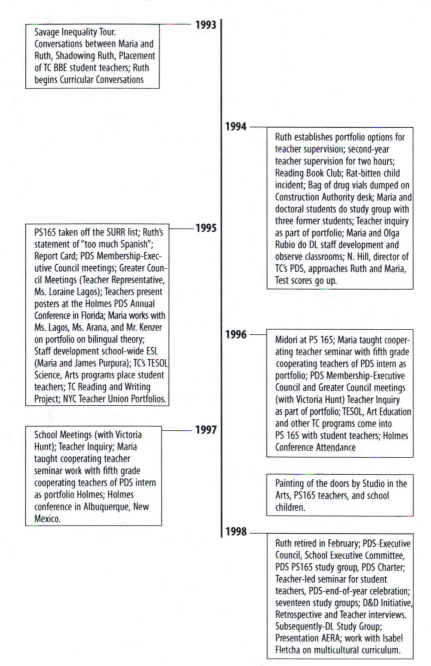

1993

Savage Inequality Tour. Conversations between Maria and Ruth, Shadowing Ruth, Placement of TC BBE student teachers; Ruth begins Curricular Conversations

1994

Ruth establishes portfolio options for teacher supervision; second-year teacher supervision for two hours; Reading Book Club; Rat-bitten child incident; Bag of drug vials dumped on Construction Authority desk; Maria and doctoral students do study group with three former students; Teacher inquiry as part of portfolio; Maria and Olga Rubio do DL staff development and observe classrooms; N. Hill, director of TC's PDS, approaches Ruth and Maria, Test scores go up.

1995

PS165 taken off the SURR list; Ruth's statement of "too much Spanish"; Report Card; PDS Membership-Executive Council meetings; Greater Council Meetings (Teacher Representative, Ms. Loraine Lagos); Teachers present posters at the Holmes PDS Annual Conference in Florida; Maria works with Ms. Lagos, Ms. Arana, and Mr. Kenzer on portfolio on bilingual theory; Staff development school-wide ESL (Maria and James Purpura); TC's TESOL Science, Arts programs place student teachers; TC Reading and Writing Project; NYC Teacher Union Portfolios.

1996

Midori at PS 165; Maria taught cooperating teacher seminar with fifth grade cooperating teachers of PDS intern as portfolio; PDS Membership-Executive Council and Greater Council meetings (with Victoria Hunt) Teacher Inquiry as part of portfolio; TESOL, Art Education and other TC programs come into PS 165 with student teachers; Holmes Conference Attendance

1997

School Meetings (with Victoria Hunt); Teacher Inquiry; Maria taught cooperating teacher seminar work with fifth grade cooperating teachers of PDS intern as portfolio Holmes; Holmes conference in Albuquerque, New Mexico.

Painting of the doors by Studio in the Arts, PS165 teachers, and school children.

1998

Ruth retired in February; PDS-Executive Council, School Executive Committee, PDS PS165 study group, PDS Charter; Teacher-led seminar for student teachers, PDS-end-of-year celebration; seventeen study groups; D&D Initiative, Retrospective and Teacher interviews. Subsequently-DL Study Group; Presentation AERA; work with Isabel Fletcha on multicultural curriculum.

extras; the school personnel had to raise funds to supplement the lives of the children and the community.

In addition to the bright-colored rugs, the walls in the hallways became public forums for the display of student work, and strings with student work hung from one corner of the classroom to the other. The library shelves were filled to the brim. The classrooms were buzzing with life and intellectual exchange. Smiles lit the eyes of children of different racial and cultural backgrounds and a polyphony of sounds filled the air. The physical changes became symbolic of what was happening intellectually and socially.

MY QUESTIONS, MY METHODS

Ruth's six-year tenure at this school was not enough time to overcome the inequalities between the schools housed in the building, to transform each grade, to do away with all the constraints, nor to deal with all the problems that ailed this school and its community. Nonetheless, there were significant strides. She had made a dent in the social consciousness of those who stayed. Many teachers were committed to the children's development and to their own. Some of the features put in place during Ruth's tenure were sustained even after several changes in leadership. This was the context and, in some ways, the outcome. What lay between this leader with a moral imperative and those wonderful, young, and unabashed faces full of joy for learning that we were beginning to see more and more frequently as time went by? What had happened in those "in-between" years? How did this school transform from a low-resource, low-performance school to a bubbling, challenging, intellectually stimulating place, and a desirable place to work?

Between the administration and the children was the school staff, particularly, the teachers. We all recognize how important the teachers' work is in guiding our future leaders and citizens, but we have not explored their work sufficiently. We speak to the need for more open spaces for student learning, but we scarcely inquire about the spaces for teachers' learning. We talk about how teachers ought to have high expectations, but we do not explore how teachers think about educational goals. We know and talk about the increased strangulation of teachers' professional autonomy but we do not explore how seeds of freedom grow in periods of heightened forms of social accountability. How could understanding some of these issues in the context of what happened at PS 165 give guidance to others who would want to engage in similar transformations in their schools? These are some of the issues that will be partially addressed in the pages ahead.

I began working with PS 165 with a set of theoretical beliefs. The first assumption concerned how to approach research in schools. I felt I had to earn the school instructional personnel's trust so that my research focus would be meaningful both to me and, ultimately, to them and the children. I have worked with teachers at this school for over ten years. However, I ground the theory-building exercise this book represents on a shorter period—the six years of Ruth's tenure. My second basic assumption was that teachers could guide educational researchers in developing improved educational theories. I was particularly interested in teachers who worked with bilingual learners and what they could contribute to the field of bilingual teaching/learning and development. The latter constitutes the camera lenses[20] through which I came to know the school. While I started with these basic assumptions and a sociocultural outlook on learning and teaching, the theoretical centering on freedom comes from my participation in this school and my ethnographic telling.

I found Amartya Sen's work on freedom catching my heart and mind, as it was not only a new way of thinking about development, but it touched a chord within me. It was something I knew all my life. A person's worth and the quality of one's life is not in how much money he or she makes. There is much more. Sen proposes that we ought to look at the levels of freedom enjoyed individually and within groups. I come from a working-class background; my father was a steel worker and my mother a seamstress and houseworker. If I had believed in money as value, I may have never believed in myself enough to become a professor at an ivy-league institution. This is key to the relationships I explore between freedom, language, culture, and education.

I found support for a more scholarly personal narrative in what two scholars proposed. The first was Christopher Brumfit in his book *Individual Freedom and Language Teaching* (2001), where he makes the point that those who are the direct benefactors of educational researchers' work—teachers—need to understand what we have to say about their lives. Simplification and accessibility of important concepts is one of educational researchers' aims, as "we have to offer categories which [they] can reject on the basis of teaching experience, without having to become self-taught and inefficient theoreticians or researchers in order to do so."[21] As I propose in other work I have published,[22] the simplification is in the presentation, not in the language or in the sophistication of ideas. I also owe much to Robert J. Nash.[23] As I read *Liberating Scholarly Writing*, where he proposes that scholarly personal narratives can be more powerful than some traditional scholarly writing styles, I gave myself permission to move into a freer, more personal style. The process as much as the outcome of this book, thus, has been about freedom for me. Development as freedom, however, is conceptually incomplete unless it also promotes freedom for others. Thus, it is my hope that those who read this book will gain an understanding of how to step into spaces of freedom for themselves.

In Chapters 2 and 3, I will identify the stories associated with the theoretical threads that weave toward a perspective on language development as freedom. Exploring the construction of professional development as a freedom are Chapters 4, 5, and 6. I move into the construction of teacher theories and practices centered on intellectual development as a freedom in Chapters 7. In the last chapters (8–11) Ruth and I reflect on the potential of the theory of development as freedom within the context of PS 165 and I finish with my own personal reflections on freedom and provide a conclusion.

ACTIVITIES

1. Think about educational stories of hope that you have heard (e.g., a nontraditional student who succeeds academically against all kinds of odds, an immigrant parent who has overcome many obstacles and managed to educate all his or her children, a teacher who has an outstanding reputation of taking failing children and assisting them in academic success, a group of children who have blossomed into academic successes despite having all the characteristics of being at risk, etc.) at home, at school, or in society. How did you find out? (Newspaper, word of mouth, TV, radio, Internet, or some other forms?). Find out more details about the story. What spin did the reporters/tellers of the story give to it? What were the key elements that were cause to hope? Given the details, what alternative stories could be told about the children you work with and what elements could be highlighted?

2. Think about children in your classroom who are not succeeding. Select one child you would like to interact with differently. Start by interviewing the child (or his/her parents) to find out how they see their learning or social behavioral problems and in what they are interested. Once you have done this, put it away and think

creatively. Remember, you have nothing to lose. Concentrate on the possibilities the case of this child may open up in your life. What might inspire this child? Write about it and share it with your friends, colleagues, parents, or other children. Notice how people react to the relationship between you and the child—what is different from how that relationship was constructed in the past? Try out a concrete activity that flows from your creativity and positions you in a new relationship with the child. Notice the difference in how the child reacts to this activity and compare it with the past. Rethink what you might have to do to improve your students' learning.

ENDNOTES

1. Sen, Amartya. *Development as Freedom.* (New York: Anchor Books, 1999).

2. Public School 165 was named after Robert E. Simon, a philanthropist and realtor in the 1930s; however, rarely did the staff or students of the school use this name. Thus, I do not.

3. These were ideas in conversations with Maxine Greene, a philosopher of education, author of *Dialectics of Freedom* (1989, Teachers College Press) and colleague of mine, in 2005.

4. King, Joyce E. "Diaspora Literacy and Consciousness in the Struggle Against Miseducation in the Black Community." *Journal of Negro Education* 61 (1992): 317–340.

5. See Appendix 1.1 Timeline of events covered within the six-year framework. Reference is to having been selected as one of 11 schools serving bilingual learners that had earned a place of excellence and would participate in the defunct Office of Bilingual Education, New York City Board of Education (now the New York City Department of Education), and Brown University, a program known as the Documentation & Dissemination Initiative. (1997–2002).

6. Some of the teachers were involved from the beginning through the end of Ruth's tenure, but not all of them. Similarly, some of the teachers were relatively new to the school when she retired.

7. While in the United States the bilingual learners are referred to as English language learners (ELLs), I think this is parochial and a misnomer. First, once outside the United States or the English-speaking world, they cannot be called English language learners because neither the dominant or the minoritized language may be English, as is the case in Spain when speaking of the Catalans or the Basque. Second, in dual-language education programs, both the dominant language and the minoritized language student populations are bilingual learners. PS 165 had primarily students who did not possess English as a second language and very few, if any, dominant-English speakers during Ruth Swinney's tenure as principal.

8. Bialystok, Ellen. *Bilingualism in Development: Language, Literacy, and Cognition.* (Cambridge, UK; New York: Cambridge University Press, 2001).

9. Reference is to John Kozol's 1967 book, *Savage Inequality,* published in New York by Crown Publishers.

10. Charles B. J. Snyder was the superintendent of school buildings for the NYC Board of Education between 1891 and 1923. He believed that buildings for learning needed to be peaceful, full of light, and airy. PS 165 was built in the middle of the West 109th Street block, away from the noise and buzz of the cross streets of Broadway and Amsterdam. It follows Snyder's H-plan design with a grand courtyard entrance. Today, there are modern playgrounds in the different external surroundings.

11. The newspaper coverage of the asbestos scandal in New York City during September and October of 1993 is extensive. Of particular interest on the broader neglect of the schools was the *New York Times* coverage on October 3, 1993.

12. Freire, Paolo. *Pedagogy of Freedom: Ethics, Democracy and Civic Courage.* (Lanham, MD: Rowman and Littlefield. 1999, p. 40).

13. Schools that have 60 percent or more of their students below standards are placed on a list of State Under Registration Review (SURR) schools in the State of New York. When placed on the list, a school is required to develop a comprehensive improvement plan and is monitored closely by the State Education Department.

14. The drug problems surrounding the school were exposed in the *New York Times,* July 3, 1994.

15. Sen, *Development as Freedom.*

16. I used minoritized language instead of the traditional language minority because I want to communicate that individuals or groups are minoritized when a characteristic or status is ascribed to them, in this case based on language, within a given social setting. The language itself, as is the case within with Spanish, may be classified in the linguistic world as a world language.

17. Midori, a violinist born in Osaka, Japan, in 1971, was officially designated a U.N. Messenger of Peace by Secretary-General Ban Ki-moon because of her work with communities around the world. PS 165 was a direct recipient of her response to the budget cuts in the 1990s that eliminated music in New York City public schools. Midori started a community initiative based on the belief that she had to facilitate access to music for all children, independent of background. For more information, see www.GoToMidori.com. Last retrieved on February 27, 2009.

18. Freeman, Rebecca. *Bilingual Education and Social Change.* (Clevedon, UK: Multilingual Matters, 1998, pp. 79–80).

19. Freeman, *Bilingual Education,* p. 81.

20. Fanselow's clarification of the difference between lens and camera lens can be found in the Introduction of Barnard, R., and M. E. Torres-Guzmán, eds., *Creating Classroom Communities of Learning.* (London: Multilingual Matters, 2008, pp. 10–11).

21. Brumfit, Christopher. *Individual Freedom and Language Teaching.* (Oxford: Oxford University Press. 2001, p. 44)

22. Torres-Guzmán, María E. "La Lecture Suivie n'est-elle *qui* Lecture Suivie [Are Read Alouds *Just* Read Alouds?] *Lettre de l'AIRDF, the International Research Association in French Didactics,* 25 (2005): 98–108.

23. Nash, Robert. *Liberating Scholarly Writing: The Power of Personal Narrative.* (New York: Teachers College Press, 2004).

PART ONE

LANGUAGE DEVELOPMENT AS FREEDOM

2

LANGUAGE AND CULTURE FROM THE PERIPHERY TO THE CENTER

Ruth and I coincided in multiple beliefs about language and its role in education. One shared belief concerned the intertwining of language and culture.[1] When we speak—how we say things, the choices of our words, the ideas we play with—we are displaying who we are and all that has historically, socially, and culturally influenced us. Thus, we refer to language sometimes when we mean both language and culture. That language development is critical to educational development is another of our shared beliefs. The language of our cultures and our times influences our ideas. Our ideas, usually expressed in language, influence our language. Language is not only one of the ways we express what we know; it also colors and is colored by our creativity.

Most importantly, we shared a belief that the greatest human and educational potential for children coming from homes where English is spoken minimally, or not at all, is embedded in bi/multilingual/multicultural education. There is ample research evidence to warrant this belief[2] despite the strong antibilingualism expressed in some of our nation's public opinion outlets.[3] Even so, we did not see all forms of bilingual education as rendering strong bilingualism and biliteracy in children. We seized on this convergence of views (not just ours, but those of others) to experiment with the enrichment dual-language education (DLE) model that was already being touted as beneficial for both minoritized and dominant-language children.[4]

Ruth was the leading expert in organizing dual-language education programs in the district, city, and state. Within a year of my arrival in New York, I had enrolled my child in the first dual-language education program in the city[5] that Ruth was administering. A substantial number of white middle- and upper-middle-class parents chose to enroll their children in the program. Latino middle- and upper-class parents, like myself, were fewer in number. At PS 165, however, the population differed. The student population in the dual-language education program came from a low socioeconomic background; there were no white students and few, if any, students other than Latinos enrolled in the early years of Ruth's tenure.[6] The student population was primarily Latino, mostly Dominican. It mirrored the national Latino bilingual learner—the shackles of deprivation abounded. The students were poor, and many were illegal immigrants. They lacked educational opportunity, adequate health services, and the like. They lacked many freedoms others enjoyed.

When Ruth arrived, the teaching staff, while committed to bilingualism, felt that the children were inferior. In their view, the children did not have language or culture. The teachers needed much professional development, or development of capabilities, in order to provide these children with the type of education they needed.

Within this chapter, I will describe the student population and explore how valuing the importance of language and culture in the lives of the students and the parents supported the educational program. I invite the reader to focus on how the principal and the teachers embraced two aspects of their work: (1) the multiple languages and cultures as key elements in organizing instruction, and (2) developing rigorous educational programming. While these two aspects may appear to be separate, as dual-language education programs may or may not be rigorous, for the dual-language education program at PS 165, the two aspects were intertwined and had to be treated as one. The question that inspired this chapter was: How did the connections between culture, language, instruction, and freedom play themselves out in the school? How did poverty play into this connection? The inquiry is bounded further in the dual-language education program, as this was the place from which I got to know the school, thus, reflecting my participation in the school and my partial knowing.

PS 165 COMMUNITY

The question of the unfreedoms of poverty is important in and of itself. At one point, after a rat-bitten child came to school, Ruth found out about the efforts of the parents to try to get the city to come and inspect some of the buildings and places their children roamed. When the city did not respond to parental efforts, Ruth realized, once again, that schools of disenfranchised communities had different responsibilities, as the playing field for lower socioeconomic communities is far from leveled. In most middle-class communities, parents raised about $100,000 per year for extras that the schools need. This was true within the district's middle- and upper-class communities. But at PS 165, as for many other low-resourced schools, the relationship with the community was turned on its head. It was the other way around. PS 165 parents needed support for their community struggles, and the school offered parental support and educational opportunities that assisted them in developing skills to advocate for themselves and their children. As a result, at PS 165 the teacher center doubled as a parent center for learning, and the school sought to support parents in many other ways.

The diversity of cultures, languages, and literacies added new elements to the power relationships associated with poverty and the differential treatment of the children. Their ability to access a better life had added difficulties. Most research on the benefits of bilingualism, according to Bialystok,[7] has been conducted with middle-class student populations. Bialystok poses the following question: "Do children who enjoy less privilege respond in the same way as those who are more favored, learning their two languages according to the same principles, and profiting from the same cognitive benefits of bilingualism where they arise?"[8]

I do not propose to address this question directly. However, the socioeconomic background of the student population and the community of PS 165 are important to understand as a contextual factor associated with their bilingualism and academic achievement. It helps explain what Ruth found upon arrival in the areas of student achievement and teacher development.

At PS 165, more than 60 percent were Latinos; in the dual-language education program within the school, the percentage of Latinos soared up to 100 percent. They were Dominican, Mexican, Puerto Rican, Honduran, Salvadoran, and other Spanish-speaking backgrounds, but the groups that were most rapidly growing were from the Dominican and Mexican groups of newcomers to New York City.[9] The majority of the students (approximately 85 percent) were dominant in Spanish, with the remaining as English dominant. When asked about her students, one of the dual-language teachers responded:

> Most of my students are Spanish dominant and all of my students are from a Hispanic background, and I myself am Spanish dominant and from a Hispanic background. So that has been a very, very positive experience with the students because I can bond with them much more easily and I can touch the different cultural aspects more easily with their native language, which is Spanish. We really have in-depth discussions in Spanish because the students are very proficient in Spanish so we have the opportunity to not only read and write in the language but really touch and tackle very advanced and critical skills used in the native language that they use the most. And, also to attend to their cultural diversity because even if we are all Hispanics, we are Hispanics of different countries, of different cultural traditions, so here, we try to enhance all those cultural diversities at a very high level.

The student population at PS 165 represented what was happening nationally. While English, the language of the United States, is the most common international language of the world and serves to engage nations worldwide in the market economy of which the United States is the quintessential exporter,[10] there are ever-growing numbers of speakers of languages other than English (LOTE) within its borders.

Major Asian languages—like Japanese, Chinese, and Korean—and Spanish are heard in the airports on the West Coast, and the European, Middle Eastern, African, and Spanish from the Caribbean are heard in many airports on the East Coast. All major cities in the United States have multilingual announcements for mass transportation, public telephones, emergency units, and the like. Some health services, by law, are to be mediated by language, and translations of key legal materials are required. Religious services are offered in a variety of languages. The non-English media—television and radio channels—is growing dramatically. Within the film and music industries, other languages' words leak in as linguistic borrowings. This multilingualism is not just a result of hospitality to the nation's visitors as tourists; much of it is the result of the close to 30 percent growth of the population in the United States due to immigration.

LATINOS

The National Clearinghouse for English Language Acquisition (NCE-LA)[11] documents an extraordinary growth in school enrollment: 65.03 percent—from 3 to 5 million—between the years of 1993 and 2004, of children from homes where the language is other than English. The general growth of the school-aged population in the nation, however, was 9.19 percent. The numbers of identified languages children come to school with were 384 in 2001; almost 80 percent of the population of non-English speakers were Spanish speaking.

Spanish-speaking populations have spread throughout the nation due to immigration and high birth rates; but there are Latinos, particularly those in the Southwest, in Florida, and on the East Coast, whose historical roots go back many generations. Some trace their ancestors as inhabitants of the territories that are now part of the United States prior to their annexation. Their families were never immigrants; some were among the early explorers. Other Latino groups are from countries that were conquered and/or annexed. The historical relationships of the different Latino groups to the United States are varied.

Despite the variation amongst Latinos, there are many long-standing skewed societal beliefs about them. For example, they are subject to "lumping." Lumping would be like saying that the languages and cultures of Australia, England, and New Zealand were one. They are not. They are distinct, although there are some aspects of the cultures that may be similar and the base of the language is the same. All individuals from Spanish-speaking backgrounds are viewed as one cohesive group, but in reality they come from 21 different countries. Frequently, all that is in common between an Argentinean and a Mexican is what appears to be the same language, Spanish, and aspects of the heritage culture. The reality is that one of the first interactional tasks in a mixed Spanish-speaking group is to negotiate meanings of the same words, to ask how you would say x in your country, or to joke about the subtle meanings of words. There is a lag in understanding the language of another Spanish-speaking group. This is not even speaking about intervening issues of class, gender, region, etc., which are also markers of differences that come into the exchanges within the Latino population. All "Latino" means, within the United States, is that the individual comes from a Spanish-speaking country.

Some people argue for the umbrella term "Hispanic" because of the historical roots of the language being from Hispania, what Spain was once called, and because "Latino" is a broader term referring to those who speak a language of Latin origin, which would include Italians, French, and the like. While I acknowledge the etymological roots of the term "Hispanic," I have preferred "Latino/a" because I grew up in a time and a place when the reference was to the U.S. historically rooted Latin American Spanish-speaking groups—the Mexican, Puerto Rican, and Cuban populations—that were in large numbers within the United States in the 1960s. In addition, "Latino" was in reference to Latin America and included the indigenous populations from Latin America who did not speak Spanish or were bilingual in their own native language and Spanish.

The heterogeneity of the Spanish-speaking population in the United States has begun to show, and the meaning of the term has extended to include all the different groups. The point here is that the group norms to which a child belongs may be difficult to determine by just saying he or she is Latino or comes from a Spanish-speaking country. The group norms, whatever they may be, differ from the mainstream cultural norms within the United States. Yet, most teachers are prepared through an idealized mainstream cultural prism. The prism includes norms that mirror and perpetuate the power relationships in our society. The minoritized Spanish-speaking children appear to be very distant from what is taught to be the norm. This knowledge wedge enters into the ways we treat children in schools.

In *Children Are Watching*,[12] Cortes proposes that common beliefs usually reflect and project the characterizations of Latinos as seen in, for example, the media. Films and news clips depict and conjure up these social beliefs in their selections of portrayals. He suggests that most social beliefs widely held amongst the average American, that is, the average principal, the average teacher, the average parent, and the average child reflect that which is presented on television. Latinos themselves internalize these social beliefs. Some even define themselves in light of in these beliefs, despite the fact that many of the characterizations verge on stereotypes.

One of the images that I have repeatedly found in conversations with school personnel in the last 30 years reappeared amongst the PS 165 teachers. The phrase "these children come to school with no language and culture" captures such a belief. Ruth, in the excerpt below that came from one of my interviews with her after she left the school, talked about the presence of these teachers' beliefs when she arrived.

It was the first meeting of the school staff. Ruth had telephoned all the teachers in the school, inviting them to come and set up their classrooms before school started by offering them breakfast. There was no tradition of this occurring as in many middle-class schools. Teachers at PS 165, when Ruth began, showed up on the first paid day of the school year. Previously, with the children in the school building, the teachers would begin to set up their classrooms. So that getting the teaching personnel to come before school started was one of the rituals of Ruth's legacy. In the first meeting with the staff that first year, the negative social belief about the children showed up. Ruth recalled:

At PS 165, the teachers ... believed that they [the children] did not have culture or language. It's as if to say, "they [the teachers] ... think or feel—they're [the children are] empty." It was a real lack of belief in—even from Hispanic teachers that were part of the community—the children and their communities. I told them that even my dog, Sancho, had a language and a culture; it was dog language and culture.[13]

I have come to understand that when teachers say, "these children come to school with no language and culture," they mean that the children do not know academic English, if they know any English at all. Furthermore, they mean that when the children speak Spanish, or any other language that is not English for that matter, it is usually not a standard Spanish and, even if it were, it is not important for schooling and testing. English is the language of standardized testing and, ultimately, of social mobility in the United States. School personnel are operating, whichever way we put it, from the belief that children have to learn to "pull themselves up by their bootstraps" and learning English is part of doing this. School personnel, when they believe children must be from a certain mold divorce themselves from the very process of the students' learning. They blame the victim and position learning within the individual and their abilities.

Many educators assume a leveled playing field and believe that by having the same expectation for all and giving the children the same treatment, often conceptualized as equity, they are doing well by the minority communities they serve. They are far from doing so.

Stereotypes, like the "children don't have culture and language," are lacking in fundamental ways. The stereotypes represent fixed way of thinking about identity. Identity of individuals within the construction of stereotypes do not reflect the everyday dynamic and situational construction of identity in our lives. We meet many people in a day and we meet these people in different circumstances—churches, schools, mass transportation, and restaurants—where we play different roles—mother, teacher, partner, and so forth. The image the individual has of him- or herself differs in the different situations. Just take an adolescent with her or his friends as opposed to who she or he is when interacting with a friend of the family. Stereotyped images are static, not dynamic enough. They do not acknowledge individual variations emerging from an individual's choice of constituting him- or herself as part (or not) of the group, or from an individual's choice of which one of the group characteristics he or she constitutes as part of self. Nor do stereotypes capture the shifts of the groups as a whole.

How Ruth worked against stereotypes came up not just with teachers but also with parents. Ruth had removed a group of parents from the school grounds on the basis that they were stifling their children's growth by hanging outside the classrooms and accompanying their children into the lunchroom, but she knew many were unemployed and she sought to employ them when it was possible. For example, when she found a city and teachers' union clause prohibiting the teachers from being assigned to lunch duty, she sought to employ some of the parents. She found a few individuals among the unemployed parent population who managed lunch duty well, so she hired them. Rather than see parents as one whole group, Ruth saw them as individuals and she built on their strengths. She was intent on positioning the school as a resource for the community despite tensions with these very same parents. The parents came to value the school community that respected and valued them. Ruth saw her parents for who they were and nudged those she had to and embraced those that she could.

What the relationship between the parents and Ruth illustrates is that while the population of parents was the same—when she asked them to leave the premises and when she asked some of them to engage productively as part of the community—each situation called for different positioning. In other words, Ruth was reinventing herself and the parents in each of the situations.[14] We constitute ourselves uniquely in each of the situations we encounter every single day of our lives. Yet when we use stereotyping in relation to others we are inhibiting a fluidity of relationships, as we do not embrace the intricacy of being "human" in others.[15] In other words, when we act upon stereotypes we are not acknowledging this human need among those whom we stereotype.

I have found in conversations with students, teachers, and people at large that an individual's experience with a Latino/a tends to mediate the camera lenses through which the individual comes to the general images they hold about others. Social beliefs may connect with how composite statistics about the characteristics of a particular ethnic or racial group are interpreted. The group prism, however, is not acceptable as a way of defining an individual. It restricts us from seeing the person and his or her humanity. The individual is more complex than what the general cultural and social tendencies of the group may be, even though some of these tendencies may be constituent parts of who he or she is. While we may know about the cautions of defining individuals through group portrayals, and while there are an increasing number of examples of how some of us challenge the stereotypes,[16] the images of groups are persistent and, at times, self-perpetuating. In schools, as social institutions, stereotypes show up regularly.

That the members of PS 165's population were, in majority, Spanish speaking was important in understanding the school personnel's views when Ruth began and what had to happen. They had to confront and counter their own images of the children and their insecurities as to whether they could bring the population "up to speed," a task that maybe not all believed they could do. Specifically, they were worried about their capacity to raise the test scores that they needed to survive as a school community. Much was done during Ruth's tenure at the school—there were some changes in beliefs and a few small miracles. Nonetheless, the testing still remains an issue, even more now that our society has accepted standardized testing as a way of making schools educationally accountable.

TEST SCORES AND TRANSFORMATION

Tests, in my view, have become a substitute for a more honest dialogue. We ought to be discussing the responsibility of the adult world in the preparation of our youth in a more forthright manner. We ought to be discussing the kind of world we are making for them to live in and make theirs. Within our society, however, testing is perhaps one of the nation's strongest icons with respect to education. In our public discourse, tests are a measure of school effectiveness. Yet, tests, as the Goodmans propose, measure the past, what has been taught, not the future or what one can imagine as possible.[17] So, how did PS165 embrace testing?

The children at PS 165 had not been doing well in tests; it was the third year the tests had gone down when Ruth arrived. The school was under close state scrutiny as the composite scores decreased with consistency. The legacy of a historical belief about the relationship between outcomes of testing and intelligence amongst Latinos[18] was not just in the past; it was coloring the views people held at PS 165, even among the Latino teachers. In other words, the national and local school discourse converged on the unquestioned assumption that the children's educational capabilities could be discussed as a correlation of the low test scores, the lack of English proficiency, and the lack of intelligence. PS 165 was barely surviving, and this legacy of beliefs had reinforced the school personnel's views on their inability to do much with the student population they taught.

The first year Ruth was a principal, the tests went down one more time. According to Ruth, there was no doubt that the school personnel knew that their survival, as a school, depended on paying attention to the test scores of the children at PS 165. The teachers themselves made distinctions between assessments, city tests, and standardized testing. Not all of the assessments and tests were viewed in negative ways. Some assessments that were being introduced toward the end of Ruth's tenure—such as the district's ECLAS, which is a way of understanding and classifying students' language and literacy needs in the lower elementary grades—the teachers recognized as useful. The utility of the assessment or test emerged when they could see the connection between the assessment and instruction and when this connection was further associated with the measurement of progress of their students. This type of evaluative tool was time-consuming, but the benefits derived from them were highly valued; they were directly tied to instruction and to the students' learning.

Standardize tests, however, were not viewed as benevolent in nature. To the contrary, they were seen as tyrannical. The reasons were various. The teachers knew they had to do test preparation. Yet, they felt it was unreasonable that to prepare students for an April test, the school would begin setting up test preparation in January. Cluster teachers[19] and teachers alike were assigned to work on test-taking skills, and this would intensify as they got closer to the actual test-taking dates. This view was neither articulated as "wasting" time nor as a resigned lament, but as a critique. Test preparation took an inordinate amount of time, and because the tests were in English, what they measured, most of the time, was no more than the child's knowledge of the English language. The tests did not predict anything. This understanding about tests was even less tolerable when a connection was made between the student scores and how teachers were valued in relation to the test. It was not just a connection made by others about teachers; it was how it influenced the teachers' view of themselves.

One of the lower-grade, dual-language teachers expressed her curiosity about how the tests created the need for professional development and its impact on the sense of self. She told me that she had experienced a good instructional year, only to be disappointed with the test scores she received at the end of the year. She was perplexed with the assumed relationship between teaching and tests. She realized that being in a situation where the children had instruction in two languages did not initially show up in a positive outcome during the students first few years.[20] She worked on acceptance of this because the self-doubt about her effectiveness as a teacher was also growing too difficult to bear when she saw the results. She felt that, despite accepting this reality of standardized testing outcomes for bilingual children, others pushed her, and she pushed herself, to seek out more help and to strive to improve her teaching.

It took some time for teachers to get to the point where they could see tests connected to the rigor of their teaching. Some teachers refused to go this route and requested transfers from the school. Within three years, about half of the teaching staff was new, which gave Ruth the opening to hire teachers who were more in line with her thinking and to help the other half rethink how to work with the children more effectively. The teachers' concern about the rigor of their teaching began to connect to the relationship of thinking, learning, and testing but was always mediated by the multiple languages of instruction.

Tests have been portrayed as assessment of knowledge and skills. Test items are usually constructed so that new problems or situations that represent the knowledge, skills, or other competencies expected of the children are chosen as test items. At least this is what the test makers say they do. Testing requires that the individual be able to abstract aspects of knowledge, that which is transmitted, and apply it to new situations or problems. This ability to transfer from one situation is what Bruner calls transferring understanding.[21] It is a type of independence in thinking: that is, the ability to transfer what you know, and what applies, to a new format. In addition, there is also knowledge and skill in test taking, and many students at PS 165 came from countries where this kind of testing was not part of their school cultures.

The teachers at PS 165 were struggling with getting the children to be socially and intellectually independent, but they knew that language was an issue key to the demonstration of knowing, especially for non-English native speakers. After much discussion, the goal the school personnel could live with was one that would move the school in ways that did away with the threat of closure while at the same time creating a space for experimenting with languages and alternative pedagogies, and that would ensure a push toward linguistic freedoms. In an interview, Ruth stated:

> We were in a dire situation because the school was on the SURR list when I took it over. It was in its third or fourth year of being on that list and in danger of being closed. So, there was a general understanding that if we didn't improve the scores in the third grade, we would no longer exist.
>
> My first year, the scores went down and I had to be very smart because for us to survive, we had to increase the scores. It was a hard decision as to where to put our efforts to do this. The state determined success by the number of kids on or above the 50th percentile on the state tests. Kids in the 0 through 10th percentile represented a lot of work, so we put our efforts into survival. We put our initial efforts into the upper 20th through 25th percentile, to move them to the 50th percentile so that they could be at another level. We also worked with the 40th through 45th percentile because they were a relatively easy push into the next level. That strategy paid off tremendously, and we moved the school out of SURR in a relatively short time.
>
> The other thing we did was test prep from almost the beginning of the year. Against all my beliefs, because this is not how I see what education is about, but we had students do practice tests, initially once a month and eventually twice a week. The focus was on skills of taking a test. We had our instructional efforts on literacy and ensured that the test prep was at another period of the day. We needed to survive and I am a pragmatic and practical person.
>
> People understood and agreed with me; there was a vested interest for all of us because the SURR status was like a brand on our chest—like the S of the Scarlet Letter. Everyone felt bad about it. We felt inferior to everyone; there was no resistance to working smartly and what this meant. It was impossible to move the 1st percentile to the 50th. I had to divide the school and work with the third and fourth grades differently. This did not mean we did not work in the other grades but we had to move kids in these grades into the 50th percentile.

One could debate Ruth's pragmatic approach on many fronts, but there was no resistance in the school or in the community. The actions in the school were cushioned by the belief amongst many Latino communities that the reason they came to the United States was for their children to obtain *una educación y una vida mejor* (a better education and a better life). For example, one parent of the dual-language program echoed some of the parental beliefs about the relationship between language and learning. She stated:

> *Todos [mis hijos] han estado en este programa. A mi me gusta esta escuela porque todos aprenden en los dos idiomas y por eso quiero que el [niño] vaya también.... A mi me gusta los dos idiomas, me gusta mejor que aprenda los dos idiomas. Yo pienso que se aprende el inglés bien y el español no se olvida. Porque si solo aprendieran solo un idioma, yo pienso que se le olvidaría su español y va a querer más el inglés. Con los dos idiomas están aprendiendo más, están progresando.* [All of my children have been in this program. I like this school because all of the kids learn two languages and that is why I want him to attend as well.... I like both languages; I prefer that they learn both. I believe that they learn English well and they do not forget Spanish. If they learned in only one language, they would forget Spanish and love English more. With both languages they learn better, they progress].[22]

Not all the parents believed in this specific connection and not all the children who were not proficient in English were in the dual-language education program, but what this parent expressed is at the heart of the connection between language and education that I wish to highlight. It also expresses caring about education. There is no doubt that Latino parents care about their children. One piece of evidence comes from the Hispanic Pew Center and the Zobgy poll on the 2004 presidential campaign. Education ranked the number one issue in determining for which candidate the Latino would vote.[23] Throughout the years, education has only been toppled once by the immigration question. It is not that the Latino wants the candidate to know Spanish, but the symbolism of the language looms high. The overwhelming majority of Latinos believed that knowing English is important for succeeding, educationally and economically, in this country. These findings do not contradict the parent's formulation above. Her beliefs that learning English ought not substitute for her children's development of Spanish reflected a key assumption underlying the beliefs developed in PS 165's dual-language education program. The school stood for not eradicating but protecting the children's native language, as knowing it made it possible for students to connect to their ancestral cultures; it allowed them to talk to their grandparents; it allowed them to bring forth aspects of their culture that they could reexamine and incorporate in their own lives. There are many ways to do this, and at PS 165 one of the most successful aspects of the school's response to the community needs was the dual-language education program. As the parent proposed: "With both languages they [the children] learn better, they progress." As the dual-language education program was the angle of the camera lenses through which I knew the school, within, I will emphasize the program, although the issues were taken up in the monolingual program because there were many children who were not proficient in English who were placed, by parental consent, in the regular English programs in the school.

PARAMETERS FOR DUAL-LANGUAGE EDUCATION

Ruth was successful in pushing for an expansion of dual-language education at the district level. PS 165 was one of the five new programs that came into existence as a result of her perseverance. As soon as she knew she would be appointed as the new principal and prior to her taking on the role, Ruth had discussed the educational issues of bilingual learners and the model of dual-language education with PS 165 teachers. A cadre of teachers was committed to developing quality education of bilingual and bicultural children and, with different degrees of enthusiasm and some hesitation, decided to transfer from a traditional transitional bilingual education model into an enrichment one. Nationally, the dual-language education model was appearing to be the most successful, achievement-wise, of the different types of bilingual education. The new principal was not only promoting it; she was a pioneer in organizing the model.

More importantly, however, the model responded to the desires of a large proportion of the Latino parent community that insisted in the value of maintaining the children's home language while learning the second language, English, or visa versa—and of maintaining and developing the second language while learning and developing the heritage language.

One of my doctoral students[24] documented how the children's knowledge of English loomed high amongst PS 165 parents' priorities, as it does nationally among Latinos according to a study of the Pew Hispanic Center.[25] Moreover, in this school, as in the nation, the majority of the Latino parents (over 88 percent in the 2004 Pew Hispanic Center Study) also believed that it was important to help students from families who spoke a language other than English at home to maintain the families' native tongue. They believed in bi/multilingualism. It, and not monolingualism, was the future. There was opportunity for learning both languages, and learning more than one language was not, in any way, construed as educationally harmful. Parental choice was part of the process.

I found some evidence of parental choice in teachers' responses to questions about school enrollment. One of the teachers pointed out that enrollment in the program was not only about entitlement but also a parental choice:

> We have students from the neighborhood who are entitled to bilingual services. This is the majority of our population. Some parents choose to place their child in a DLE setting to develop their Spanish.

Ruth's conceptualization of the 50/50 language allocation DLE model was value driven. It was a form of language equity.[26] She upheld language equity as a value, similar to the value-driven principle that Keyes, Hanley-Maxwell, and Capper[27] described in a study on a successful disabilities program. In Ruth's experience, successful implementation of dual-language education programs in the school district required a consistency in language policy and she was willing to set the parameters for this to occur at PS 165.[28] For Ruth, language equity was the bottom line. Ruth would not tolerate any violation of what she upheld as language equity, but there was some flexibility in the way it was implemented. Later, we will focus on the relationships between bottom line and flexibility. Here, we will highlight some of Ruth's associated values.

Ruth had a discourse of academic excellence and rigor in dual-language education and in education in general. In Spanish and English, the word *rigorosa* ["rigorous"] can mean both severity and strictness, but it can also mean thoroughly accurate or exact scholarship. Out of Ruth's mouth it took on the latter sense; it meant that teachers, while attending to language allocation, had to go beyond language. They had to look at the quality of instruction and the richness and complexity of languages used. Freire refers to this as ethical rigor.[29]

Ruth encouraged and challenged the school teaching staff to let go of haphazard ways of teaching language minority students, which she liked to call "linguistic chaos." What she considered chaotic was the inconsistency seen in many bilingual education programs where each teacher decides the language allocation. What was occurring was that each teacher had her own views of what ought to occur. Thus, a child could attend a kindergarten where the medium of instruction was Spanish, then a first grade in which the instruction was all in English, and then a second grade where instruction took place in a mix of the two languages. Such a child would then arrive at the third grade, where he or she would be tested in academic language without a strong foundation in either Spanish or English.

Instead, Ruth advocated for teachers to take up the centrality of language in a serious and systematic manner as a whole school or program. At PS 165, the dual-language education program had engaged in what Ruth called "language mapping," where the group of teachers in the program designed instruction and language allocation so that each language was supporting the children's language and academic development. There were many aspects to language mapping, as language was central but not the only factor considered. For example, a staffing decision associated with language allocation was the institution of team teaching in the dual-language education program at all but the kindergarten through first-grade levels. Within the context of team teaching, Ruth felt teachers could make clearer decisions about how to separate languages for instruction and how to bring together the content within each of the languages.

Team teaching was showing promise in the other schools with dual-language education programs in the district. It is a structure requiring close collaboration and strong communication between teachers. By choosing team teaching as a basic structure that would facilitate carrying out the theoretical framework of the language-based model, the program was constituted around collaboration. Within this book, teachers' views on collaboration will be further revealed. Here, I quote two teachers who expressed their views on the organization and support provided by the teaching teams.

Teacher #1: Team teaching from the second to fifth grades has been a very effective structure for academic instruction. Each teacher is responsible for only one language; each teacher has her own room. This keeps the separation of both languages in their own context (PS 165 teacher; written response to survey, 1999).

Teacher #2: I teamed up with another teacher. So, I taught the Spanish component and the other teacher taught the English component. This structure helped us a lot in this new program [dual-language education] that was being implemented in the school because we had a lot of meetings to talk about the curriculum and to develop the different ways that we were going to work. We also dealt with how we were going to divide the curriculum and what aspect each was responsible for covering. So, the structure helped us a lot. Also, the school administration gave us a lot of support for these teams because we had common preps so we could talk (PS 165 teacher, interview, 1999).

Accompanying the social separation of languages through team teaching, or the planned diglossia—where each language has a distinct social space—was the need for "academic rigor." Looming over the school was the threat of the state takeover. The threat facilitated Ruth's call for teachers to have high expectations for the children, to make the learner the center of instruction, and to create consistency in instructional practices throughout the grades.

Simultaneously, there were other collaborative structures, like grade level, program, and schoolwide meetings, that came into existence. All of them helped shape the schoolwide ethos around collaboration for which the school was to be known when Ruth left. It was in this collectivization, or community building, that the teachers began to voice various needs—the need for schoolwide policies that supported the dual-language education program, the need for a consistent academic language, and the need for program and school curriculum alignment across and within grade levels. The general call for academic rigor, thus, went beyond the dual-language education program. Academic rigor and collaboration were both constituent aspects, and context of, the program. The collaborative structures supported integration of the program in the school, as it gave the teachers the opportunity of voicing the need for greater understanding of the complexity in their work schoolwide.

The separation of languages that had been adapted initially in the PS 165 dual-language education program was the alternate day approach, where one language was the medium of instruction one day and the second language would be the medium of instruction the following day, what Garcia[30] calls the alternate day compartmentalization. At the end of a ten-day period, the teacher teams would reassess how the amounts were actually distributed, accounting for special events, unpredictable occurrences, and so forth, and make adjustments, if necessary, in their planning. In other words, if there had been many interruptions in the designated Spanish days, they would start with Spanish the coming week. Since there were team teaching structures starting in second grade, where one teacher was the designated Spanish teacher and the other the English teacher, they had to evaluate the weeks for both groups of students and look for ways to adjust both classes. The teaching team made these decisions every two weeks.

In summary, the program's theoretical framework, particularly those aspects of consistency in language policies, language separation, and language and content integration created, in practice, the necessity for collaboration. Accompanying collaboration was a deep commitment to improve the quality of the program and to engage in academic rigor. At PS 165, the conversations about dual-language education that began while Ruth was the district coordinator for such programs were extended when she became the school principal. With the conversation about language and academically rigorous instruction, she also brought in the collaborative structures such as team teaching. Collaboration, which began with a cadre of teachers in the dual-language education program, was extended to the entire school and became critical to the school's future.

REFLECTION ON UNFREEDOMS

In this chapter, I have focused on the unfreedoms of poverty, meaning the lack of access to basic needs such as shelter and food, and to the unfreedom of education, meaning that the conditions were full of obstacles in the students' path toward reaching their full potential. There were also the unfreedoms generally imposed by testing, as many schools are placed in situations where the curriculum for improving test scores is prescribed. While the district was pushing PS 165 and Ruth to improve the language proficiency scores and the standardized test scores, the curriculum standards were available only to the English component of the program. The Spanish component had no prescribed curricula.

As Ruth took a value-driven approach to her leadership, she guided the teachers towards language equity. There were some freedoms established in relation to the languages of instruction. This was important for she established the context of the dual-language education teaching and learning. Ruth was also clear that she did not want the instruction in the two languages to be done haphazardly. She wanted teachers to be systematic and rigorous in their use of language within instruction. In future chapters, I will focus more on the core of the practices and beliefs of the teachers of the program. In the next chapter, we will explore how the teachers stepped into freedom within the context of the bottom line Ruth posed.

ACTIVITIES

1. Look at data on the Latino population in your city. What do they tell you? Interview three to five parents to find out what their aspirations for their children are, how they see the schools leading their children to those goals, and where they could be doing better. Compare what you thought when you looked at the statistics with what the parents tell you. What have you learned about in the process?

2. If there are dual-language education programs in the city, go to one of the schools implementing the program. Interview the administrator and a few teachers to find out the model. Find out who the students are from a language standpoint—do they speak English or are they speaking a language other than English? How is the language allocated? By teacher? By subject? What are the factors they consider important for their model?

ENDNOTES

1. Goodenough, Ward H. "Culture, Language, and Society." *Module in Anthropology,* 7 (1971): 1–48. MA: Addison-Wesley. Goodenough proposes that culture is carried primarily in the semantic and symbolic aspects of the languages. Both language and culture are juxtaposed and intertwined in cognitive, intellectual, academic, affective, and other processes in education that, in turn, mirror that which is occurring in society at large.

2. Thomas, Wayne, and Virginia Collier. *A National Study of School Effectiveness for Language Minority Students' Long-term Academic Achievement.* (Santa Cruz, CA, and Washington, DC: Center for Research on Education, Diversity and Excellence, 2002). Available at: http://wwww.crede.ucsc.edu/research/llaa/1.1 Last accessed on March 17, 2005; Greene, Jay P. "Metaanalysis of the Rossel and Baker Review of Bilingual Education Research." *Bilingual Research Journal* 21 (1997, 2/3). Retrieved February 5, 2002, from http://brj.asu.edu/archives/23v21/articles/art1.html. Last retrieved January 7, 2009; Ramirez, J. David, S. D. Yuen, and D. R. Ramey. *Executive Summary, Final Report: Longitudinal Study of Structured English Immersion Strategy, Early-exit and Late-exit Transitional Bilingual Education Programs for Language Minority Children. Final Report to the U.S. Department of Education* (Executive Summary and Vols. 1 and 2). (San Mateo, CA: Aguirre International, 1991).

3. Crawford, James. *At War with Diversity: U.S. Language Policy in an Age of Anxiety.* (Clevedon, UK: Multilingual Matters, 2001).

4. For more information, see Lindholm, K. J. *Directory of Bilingual Immersion Programs: Two-way Bilingual Education for Language Minority and Majority Students.* (Los Angeles, CA: University of California. Center for Language Education and Research. 1987). Lindholm, Katherine J., and Z. Aclan. "Bilingual Proficiency as a Bridge to Academic Achievement: Results from Bilingual/Immersion Programs." *Journal of Education,* 173 (1991). 99–113; Lindholm, Katherine J., and H. H. Fairchild. "Evaluation of an Elementary School Bilingual Immersion Program," in Amado M. Padilla, H. H. Fairchild, and Concepcion M. Valadez (eds.), *Bilingual Education: Issues and Strategies.* (Newbury Park, CA: Sage Publications, 1990, pp. 126–136).; Peregoy, S. F., and O. Boyle. "Second Language Oral Proficiency Characteristics of Low, Intermediate, and High Second Language Readers. *Hispanic Journal of Behavioral Sciences* 13 (1991): 35–47.

5. PS84, the Lilliam Weber School, housed the first dual-language education in the City of New York. See Crawford, James. *Bilingual Education: History, Politics, Theory, and Practice.* (Trenton, NJ: Crane Publishing Company, 1989).

6. Marquez-Lopez, Teresa. *Parental Views on Participation, Dual-language Education, and Bilingualism.* Doctoral Dissertation, Teachers College, Columbia University, 1998.

7. Bialystok, Ellen. *Bilingualism in Development: Language, Literacy, and Cognition.* (Cambridge, UK: Cambridge University Press, 2001).

8. Bialystok, *Biligualism in Development,* p. 221.

9. Torres-Guzmán, Maria E., and Stella Morales. *A Profile of Dual-Language Programs in New York City: A Subset of Six Stable Programs.* (New York: City Board of Education, 2003).

10. Calvet, Louis-Jean. *On Language Wars.* (Oxford: Oxford University Press, 1998).

11. NCELA 2004–2005 Poster. Available at http://ncela.gwu.edu/stats/2_nation .htm. Last accessed January 6, 2009.

12. Cortes, Carlos. *The Children Are Watching.* (New York: Teachers College Press, 2000).

13. Interviews with Ruth Swinney from February through June 2004.

14. Freire, Paulo. Pedagogy of Freedom: Ethics, Democracy, and Civic Courage (Lanhan, MD: Rowman and Littlefield, 2001).

15. I touch on many points and I move back and forth between them sometimes. In my discussions with teachers balancing many different roles and dealing with scores of students on a minute-by-minute basis, the interweaving and moving from one point to another is natural. And so with personal narrative writing—it reflects the way people in real situations think about things and talk about them

16. Torres-Trueba, Henry. *Latinos Unidos: From Cultural Diversity to the Politics of Solidarity.* (Lanham, MD: Littlefield Publishers, 1999); Nieto, Sonia. *Language, Culture, and Teaching: Critical Perspectives for a New Century.* (Mahwah, NJ: Lawrence Erlbaum Associates Publishers, 2002).

17. Goodman, Yetta M., and Kenneth S. Goodman. "Vygotsky in a whole-language perspective" in L. Moll (ed.) *Vygotsky and Education: Instructional Implications and Application of Sociohistorical Psychology.* (New York: Cambridge University Press, 1990, pp. 223–250).

18. Valencia, Richard. *Chicano School Failure and Success.* (London: Routledge/ Falmer, 2002).

19. According to the New York City Department of Education, cluster teachers are "all teachers who teach but do not have a homeroom and are not a Special Needs teacher," p. 10 of "Entry of Table of Organization Attributes" retrieved on February, 27, 2009, from http://school.nyc.gov/NR/rdomlyres/25FC9B28-70AD-496B-886B-065074D86D77/40987/TOInst04.pdf.

20. Thomas and Collier, *A National Study of School Effectiveness.*

21. Bruner, Jerome S. *The Culture of Education.* (Cambridge, MA: Harvard University Press, 1996).

22. Hunt, Victoria. "Intervisitation: For Professional Growth and Teacher Training." n.d.

23. Pew Hispanic Center. Hispanics and the 2004 Election: Population, Electorate and Voters (2004). Available at http://pewhispanic.org/topics/index .php?ReportID=48. Last accessed on January 7, 2009.

24. Marquez-Lopez, *Parental Views.*

25. Pew Hispanic Center, Hispanics and the 2004 Election.

26. There is some debate on whether a 50/50 language allocation is equitable, given that the overwhelming outside world is in English. Thus, there are those that advocate for more native language. Within the context of the PS 165 community, however, equal time to each of the languages was considered language equity.

27. Keyes, M. W., C. Hanley-Maxwell, and C. A. Capper. "'Spirituality? It's the core of My Leadership': Empowering Leadership in an Inclusive Elementary School. *Educational Administration Quarterly, 35* (1999): 203–237.

28. Consistency in educational practices had been found to be important for positive student educational achievement in bilingual and ESL instructional programs. See New York City Board of Education. 2000. ELL Subcommittee on Research Studies on ELLs: Progress Report. Retreived September 2007 from http://schools .nyc.gov/daa/reports/ELL_Research_Studies.pdf; Mora, J. Wink, and D. Wink. "Dueling Models of Dual-Language Instruction: A Critical Review of the Literature Review and Program Implementation Guides." *Bilingual Research Journal,* 25 (2001): 435–460; Torres-Guzmán, María E., Tatyana Kleyn, Stella Morales-Rodriguez, Stella, and Annie Han. 2005. "Self-Designated Dual-Language Programs: Is There a Gap Between Labeling and Implementation?" *Bilingual Research Journal,* 29 (2005): 453–474.

29. Freire, Paulo. *Pedagogy of Freedom.*

30. Garcia, Ofelia. "Lost in Transculturation: The case of Bilingual Education in New York City," in M. Putz, Joshua A. Fishman, and Neff-Van Aertselaer (eds.) *Along the Routes to Power: Exploration of the Empowerment Through Language.* (Berlin: Mouton de Gruyter. 2006, pp. 157–178).

3

NEGOTIATING LANGUAGE

⤝

By the second year of Ruth's tenure there was some discontent with the alternate day compartmentalization at some grade levels. The teachers had identified items that complicated their instructional environment, such as the fragmentation of their schedules with enrichment programs, programmed cluster teachers during prep time who were not bilingual, and schoolwide activities.

I learned about the teacher discontent from a small group of teachers with whom I worked and whom I will later describe. When Ruth and I spoke about it, she asked me to facilitate a discussion in the fall of the third year. I, with another colleague, Olga Rubio,[1] who had been shadowing Ruth during her second year, became the staff developers who would facilitate the language allocation discussion. There were many elements to this topic, as we would discover.

The discussion facilitated the teachers' choices with respect to language allocation while they were reexamining their beliefs. Teachers spoke to the issues of language—language equity and social justice—the validity of their work as language equity planners, the issues of freedoms and social responsibility to each other, and the creation of a school learning community. In this chapter, the focus is on the first dual-language education staff development meeting on language allocation that I attended. I will analyze it from the standpoint that decision making is not completely rational.[2] I approach the analysis of decision making as a social process anchored in our identities, our relationships, and our circumstances.[3]

From the very beginning of the discussions about dual-language education, the teachers agreed that they would not make decisions about overall language allocation on their own. They agreed that the individual decisions had social and academic consequences for their own teaching, the children's learning, and ultimately the community's aspirations for the future and the morale and functionality of the school. As a group, however, they could revisit the specific ways in which the language allocation affected groups of children and make new decisions about the ways they were allocating the language. This was the central issue of the first staff development meeting with the PS 165 dual-language education teachers. The collaboration I observed in the decision making in this meeting would cement a way of operating that offered me an understanding of freedom that I had not consciously considered before. It was critical to understanding the conceptual framework of development as freedom, and how language was central.

NEGOTIATING SPACES

The dual-language education teachers were released from their teaching duties and, with substitutes in place, they embarked in creating a programwide community and a vision for PS 165.[4]

What were their concerns and what issues did they want to discuss? What were the substantive questions that would accompany an introduction of themselves and their history at PS 165? That is how we set it up. We assumed the posture of both expert and helper. I perceived myself and other staff developers as outsiders who were the experts in bilingual/bicultural education, but the teachers' local knowledge of the school, the students, the parents, and the neighborhood was the contextual expertise that would make the discussion productive. Our different understandings Cole would call distributed.[5] I believe they were complementary.

The teachers welcomed our invitation to come to the table in a less hierarchical format and their questions emerged in an organic way. The work Ruth had already begun was obvious to me as an outsider of the school. The teachers raised, responded, and worked through the different questions emerging in their mist. They framed some of the questions in ways that could be resolved relatively quickly but most would continue as themes throughout, and to this day, power some of their conversations.

The language and cultural statuses of the minoritized language and its speakers, as opposed to English, was amongst the first to emerge. One of the seasoned teachers stood up. She gave her history at PS 165 and spoke extensively about social justice and the national bilingual education debates of the times.[6] She qualified her statements in her belief that "these debates negatively affect the school, and its functioning." She was connecting with what was going on in the larger community and the antibilingualism movement. She described the rage she and her colleagues felt about the negative press toward bilingual education. This rage had prompted two teachers into action. They wrote to the editors of one of the city newspapers, questioning the intentions of their one-sided coverage of the debates. The teacher's message to the group was that everyone played a role in establishing the status of the language. "We," she stated, "have the responsibility in the school to do advocacy work for bilingual students." The teachers admitted that their letter seemed to be ignored, but quickly added, with great conviction, that this would not stop them. "We want to make a difference in the world of the children and their communities; we see our job as doing so."

As I thought about what happened, I realized that it was also a question posed to me and my colleague—Who were we to be there with them when they were making such important decisions about their work life? We were coming from an Ivy League institution. Where did we stand? Could they trust us?

In other words, there were different planes in which we negotiated. One responded to the moment and the accomplishment of the goal of revisiting language allocation in the dual-language education program, but we were also negotiating our future as a group, and the future of our joint work in the school.

I affirmed the teachers by making an explicit connection with Cummins's[7] exhortation that teachers be advocates. It was both an occasion to say where I stood and to move them into focusing on their questions as the teachers of bilingual children at PS 165. The following were the questions we constructed together:

What are the educational rights of children who do not possess English proficiency and how do we ensure that we are doing what we can to ensure social justice? How do we determine language equity in our situation? How do we make conscious choices about the language? What are the available resources to sustain the choices we make? What do we need to enrich the Spanish component and to determine appropriately the domains of language use?

These questions were not new to me, as I had already worked with bilingual teachers for many years. They mirrored questions raised by teachers in multilingual school situations in the United States and elsewhere.[8]

One of my realizations, however, was how much the question of instructional materials related to language equity. I had often heard the lack of Spanish materials mentioned by teachers and I usually attributed this concern to the never-ending desire that most teachers have for materials they can use in their classrooms to help children learn. What I understood very poignantly in this situation was that how the teachers formulated the question about materials instantiated their questions about the issue of equity. They saw the difference in availability of instructional material in the two languages as impinging on their ability to communicate linguistic equity to their children.

The teachers were voicing the effects of what Amerin and Peña[9] referred to as asymmetry in resources and how on a daily basis this favored English in a gamut of ways. They were also responding to some of Ruth's public statements that some bilingual programs were teaching "too much" Spanish—statements that were not only disturbing to the teachers but to the bilingual community at large.[10] I later learned why Ruth would make those statements. I found evidence of the perception of "too much Spanish" in a teacher's thinking about the difference between bilingual models many years later. She spoke about what existed before and after Ruth took office.

> With the dual-language education program, you move ahead.... If you want to learn and keep your own language, I think that is the way to do it.... People can choose whether they want to be in it or not.... Every time you do something you figure out what you did wrong.... [In the program before] they [the teachers] thought that it would be a good way because kids were coming in and they were learning. [Students] didn't understand English, so they [teachers] went back to teach them in Spanish. And they did not realized it wasn't effective either.... [If it is] just going back to the native tongue, you do not really learn English.

In the meeting, the teachers were rhetorical and concrete in their questions. They were speaking from the perspective of their teaching environments while naming the obstacles and constraints they faced as they made their choices. I found them implicating themselves in the problems they faced: Given the constraints on us as teachers, how do we make language equity happen? What are our restraints and freedoms?

I saw this group of teachers embarking on an inquiry on the centrality of the issues of language development and language instruction. Yet, their concerns about language, equity, and social justice were not solely about the needs of the children and their communities, the question implicated them as the teachers and the validity of their work. The implications of language equity for those who raise it as a question began to intrigue me.

The teachers began to unpack their queries about how to make the dual-language education programmatic structure and instructional practices live up to what they proposed to be theoretically. In doing so, the question of recruiting minoritized language student populations was brought up as a way of bridging the educational and social gaps between Spanish-dominant and native English-dominant students. One of the issues that dual-language education raises is about the student population. The optimum language modeling proposed is when there are native language speakers of each of the languages. For non-English speakers to learn English, the modeling of English by native speakers is important. For the English speaker, the non-English native language speakers are important. In most of the dual-language education literature, English native speakers are usually assumed to be Euro-American, not culturally, linguistically, or racially minoritized children. Many scholars raise the issue of student population. Whom did PS 165 serve, and what questions were raised by who they were? Whom did they want to serve?

The responses of the teachers indicated where they felt grounded and where they were a bit shaky. In our conversation, the teachers, for example, affirmed their beliefs in enrichment, inclusion, equity, and social justice, and the need for the different populations to work side by side to promote cross-cultural tolerance and respect. At the same time, they reaffirmed, as a group, the need to protect and preserve the minoritized language, in this case Spanish, as a way to ensure linguistic and educational equity. Ruth was the one to voice the question at which some of them were really hinting. How do we ensure academic rigor and bilingualism with the population of our school community who lives with all the unfreedoms poverty brings with it? How do we raise the test scores to survive and go beyond that? Would it not be appropriate to speak to the recruitment of more English-speaking language models? Ruth response was:

> We do not need the white population to create an excellent program. Perhaps, it is the other way around. We will attract more white, English-speaking families as we create excellent programs.

She brought up an underlying situation within the program—that many of the students were from one of the Spanish language groups—but she also refocused the conversation on the quality of instruction that English-dominant students could provide to something more doable with what they did have and directed the discussion on what teachers could do about it themselves. I observed the teachers picking up on Ruth's discourse almost as a cue to move to the discussion of considering their responsibility for language rigor by raising a question about their instructional language policy. The teachers wanted to examine what they already knew through experience about the 50/50 dual-language model and to consider alternatives with respect to implementing it at each grade level. This was the reason we were together.

Again, the framing of the questions was significant. Another way in which the issue of asymmetry of languages showed up concretely was in the connections teachers were making between rigor and their survival as a school. The central tension they faced was anchored in the relationship between the coercion of English, as the language of testing and the freedom of the medium of instruction that bilingualism provided. Bilingualism, for the children they served, provided access to school knowledge and to learning and thinking. It was in the school that many of the children would learn to explore, to expand, to make theirs the legacy of knowledge handed down from prior generations. It was there that many of the children would learn how to struggle with personal and social freedoms. There was, in the teachers' minds, however, much more leeway for the English component of the dual-language education program to meet their tasks as they had more materials, the staff development was in English, and the support staff was primarily English speaking. They illustrated their points by identifying the underlying language-planning issues as both pedagogical and organizational.

Contrasting their present position with a recent yet faint past, the teachers expressed embarrassment that they were complaining about the riches of their enrichment programs, for example. They sounded like they were complaining about the New York Philharmonic and the studio in the School Art Program. They were not. The teachers explained that the programs were exceptional and enriching opportunities for the children. Their focus was on the issue of integration of these outside resources in instructional areas within the context of establishing language equity.

The teachers were concerned about ensuring the proper implementation of the language distribution of the model and the adequacy of time and flexibility in scheduling. The enrichment and support staff members were English speaking, and this fact posed complications for keeping the 50/50 balance in language distribution. The language of instruction of cluster teachers and better scheduling around enrichment programs were organizational issues. The teachers felt they were administrative, not curricular issues. Thus, they put them squarely back on Ruth's lap. They expressed the need for more bilingual staff and wanted to hear from Ruth how she would recruit new staff.

The outcome of this part of the discussion was an explicit resolution. The teachers affirmed themselves in their role as curriculum planners. They were the ones who would make decisions about the curricular match with the enrichment and outside activities. Ruth agreed to provide them with a menu of possible enrichment activities from which to choose at the beginning of the year, in a group format and across the grades. The teachers would discuss the menu of options to take into account the variety of needs of the children represented in the enrichment programs. Ruth also agreed to consider bilingualism as one of the criteria in hiring new staff or bringing in new enrichment programs. In other words, the teachers negotiated to ensure an environment that would sustain their choices by asking Ruth to facilitate and broaden their human and material resources through administrative action.

LANGUAGE ALLOCATION

The negotiations of how to work together, and how each had a distinct role, led to a more comfortable discussion of how they could "play" with the equity issue as they considered language allocations to meet their students' needs. One of the specific issues was that when the class was composed of primarily Spanish-dominant students, the alternate day model, where the whole day of instruction was in English, resulted in many discipline problems. The teachers from the upper elementary grades were more vocal as their lunch period was late in the day.

This is where we, as facilitators, took on a more active role. We helped them think through alternatives. The teachers concluded that two grades were going to try what they named the 50/50 roller-coaster model, also known as a serpent model, or what Garcia[11] calls the alternate teacher compartmentalization. What this meant was that the students would start the day with one language, and after lunch, they would change to the second language. The next day, the students would start with the language that they had in the afternoon of the previous day.

The excitement about this new structure was that the teachers envisioned some of the management dissipating while ensuring the separation of languages during the instructional day. One of the envisioned advantages was that it would facilitate the psychological separation of languages for the students because it would help resolve organizational and pedagogical issues around homework.

Teachers spoke about how homework in a particular language would not have to wait two days for them to see it. In the new structure, the teachers envisioned themselves as able to check on the homework the next day. They felt this would also help the children with the confusion of the language of homework notebooks. It would free them from having to keep track and remember which homework was in what language. The language of the notebook and the homework would be determined by the ending language of the day.

In addition to the psycholinguistic issues related to separating the languages, the teachers felt that the roller coaster, or serpent, model would help them better deal with language equity issues related to literacy development. It was not the traditional alternate day model with the mornings in one language and the afternoons in the other. The continuation of the language of the afternoon the next morning would place the development of literacy in both languages at the time when the students were more open to learning, in the morning.

In the lower grades, kindergarten and first grade, teachers would continue with the alternate day model. They were not in teams because of the young children's psychological issues around attachment. They were sole teachers with self-contained classrooms in which language was alternated based on time and content on a daily basis.

The old and the new structures would coexist for a period, as the upper grades chose to go with the alternate teacher compartmentalization, whereas the lower grades decided to stay with an alternate day. Ruth asked the teachers to agree that whichever specific allocation structure was adapted at a grade level would require discussion between the teacher team involved, communication with the administrator and other teachers in the program, and consistency in implementation. The language allocation, thus, would be the following for the next few years:

Box 3.1: Language Distribution and Allocation at PS 165

Kindergarten and First Grade—Same Teacher Alternating Days

Second and Third Grade—50/50 Roller Coaster/Serpent Structure

Fourth and Fifth Grade—50/50 Alternating Days

Eventually, the teachers would develop ways of planning that facilitated the language allocation structures that they chose and where they covered the content required by the state curriculum mandates. Some of the teachers explained how these different structures came together in the classroom:

Teacher #1: One teacher's instruction is in English, while the other's is in Spanish. The two classes are organized in a roller coaster model, so it's truly as 50/50 as we can get. Content areas are shared. This year the Spanish component took care of social studies the first semester and the English component did science. This semester the Spanish component does science, and English is doing social studies. Communication arts and math are planned together. Art and music take place through the Philharmonic Music Program and the studio in the School Art Program.

Teacher #2: We plan all curricula together to build on skills and concepts (no repetition in other language). We then split science in Spanish, swapping with social studies.

Teacher #3: The students understand that they have one teacher for English and another for Spanish. We feel that this separation of languages by teacher helps them to learn more and keep the languages distinct in their minds.

Teacher #4: The school has a program that focuses on making the distinction, clear distinction between the languages and developing literacy both for English and Spanish, but providing a teacher for each of the languages. From what I have noticed, I think this is probably a better model, to have two teachers. Basically, because the kids really see the distinction between the two languages as opposed to the self-contained classroom where the kids do a lot more code switching; they go from one language to the other more frequently.

This first staff development meeting was significant in that the language planning that occurred as the teachers considered the program linguistic allocation structure was based on the teachers' and the principal's beliefs and understanding of the centrality of language to the learning of the children. It was a discussion specific to the school's student population needs that, at the same time, illustrated two broader issues. The first is that language issues are not isolated; they are grounded in organization, politics, demographics, development, and the like. More and more examples are becoming available to teachers about these complexities, as people document what they do and why they do it.[12] The second is that teacher talk is also about how they see themselves in their worlds. At that time, PS 165 teachers did not have the advantage of a literature that would provide descriptions upon which to make decisions. The teachers knew they had to invent. Thus, one of their questions at this first meeting was whether "it was possible to create a vision if they did not even know what blocks they were about to use." Antonio Machado, in his poem, *Cantares*,[13] proposed that "paths are created as we walk them." By acknowledging their pioneering status, they committed themselves to walk the paths they would create. Eventually, they came to understand that even with multiple accounts of dual-language education program implementation, teachers would still have to find the spaces and processes for thinking and rethinking what is best, given their resources, their changing staff, and their changing student populations. Specific situations are contexts for specific choices.

Establishing a common vision on ways of working through issues did not box in teachers. On the contrary, it established a way of being in freedom of expression and of choosing within their community. Sharing their concerns, their ideas, and their expertise were all part of the process. There was excitement with the new-found freedom within their commitment to be consistent with the model. Their district had been innovative with respect to the education of minoritized language students, and they had the pioneer in dual-language programming in New York City as their principal—this was a great place to be. They were also becoming pioneers, as they were continuing to develop the dual-language education model. Their pioneer status provided them the freedom of standing in leadership. Their focus would no longer be how much to teach in one language or the other. This was a discussion behind them as they reembraced the 50/50 model. How language and instruction intertwined and how language specifically supported or inhibited a specific area of learning were amongst the new areas of inquiry.

Establishing these new questions of future inquiry and understanding that all questions could be revisited, the teachers concluded with a request of each other. In this request, I saw them engaging in the transformation of what was and what they envisioned. As the teachers envisioned a future, they foresaw the difficulties, and one of the teachers voiced how she would like to see the group working. She stated: "The process is going to be cumbersome and difficult at times, we need to be tolerant with each other." They were about to embark in clarifying their vision to ensure a better educational opportunity for the children they served. The teachers all agreed.

REFLECTION ON DEFINITIONS OF FREEDOM

Freedom issues appear in many instances within the these first three chapters. The most salient was the choice the school faced between the freedom to instruct children in two languages, while the test would be of the language and cognitive development of the children as demonstrated in only one—generally the weaker language of the two. In addition, this question was leaning on the substantive unfreedoms the student and community population faced. How this manifested in the school, however, were in the questions related to the unfreedoms of inequity in language—how could teachers of the non-English component compete when at the starting point—given the student population, the lack of materials, and their own lack of capability—they already experienced unequal planes?

The teachers rightfully wanted to create a new game where the fields were more leveled but they wanted to know that if they freed themselves of their stereotyped beliefs or the prism of mainstream cultural norms and took the risky steps of creativity and/or the responsibility of controlling the curriculum within the context of bilingualism, that there would be support for them amongst their peers and their superiors. This was a significant questions for the teaching personnel. How could they move children into the freedom of learning when the social and organizational structures inhibited and obstructed their access to learning?

Freedom is not a lofty or abstract concept. We make many daily decisions in which we redefine freedom personally, for groups, and for our society. Sometimes the personal, group, and societal planes come together. Where they do, we have to also make decisions about our responsibilities to each other and for the better good. An instance of the latter occurred when the teachers made the decision about accepting the 50/50 model as a bottom line, proceeding to decide on the language allocation distribution per grades. The teachers gave up their freedom to make their own individual decisions at every grade for a group and school decision on language allocation. One freedom gave way to another; all for the better good of the children. Teachers were freed from the individual decision making that seems to engender much discussion and take up a lot of time in many schools. The time and effort usually expended on this question of language distribution could then be veered towards the issues of academic rigor, that is, instructional matters, which we will explore in later chapters. The teachers were able to move in this direction because they had the support of the administration and did not live in fear of a lack of institutional freedom to use the two languages for instruction. There was a trust in Ruth's commitment to bilingualism. They had arrived at what Maxine Greene calls freedom personally realized within subjectivities.[14] Thus, freedom is not unabridged and unbounded. Freedom lives in contexts, through identities, and in specific circumstances. It is dynamically defined and redefined anew every time it is encountered.

In other words, side by side at PS 165 there were conflicting views about children as "empty" or as capable, while at the same time there was an affirmation of cultural and linguistic diversity and the need for bilingualism. The affirmation may have come from an ideological stance[15] or from an experiential understanding. Whatever its origins may have been, all the teachers had to take a stance; most accepted Ruth's bottom line.

Given the nation's preoccupation with waste in government spending, the economy, and the increase of immigrants, what was happening in this school, and in many others around the nation, has sparked many debates around the use of native languages, other than English, in schools.[16] The voting public has not been convinced that the ability to remove linguistic constraints, such as the lack of understanding of the language of instruction, provides the students who speak more than one language the ability to learn and to understand. What would motivate the principal and the teachers to jointly negotiate to stand more firmly on the freedom to use the native language for instruction? How did they move to make connections between the embodiments of this linguistic freedom and learning a reality in their school? How could they withstand the external pressures that called for abandoning the use of the native language?

It was in the words of the parent that we find an answer: *With both languages they learn better, they progress.* In her very thoughtful book on the relationship of language and cognition, Bialystok[17] suggests that the reason why teachers may intuitively, intellectually, and experientially understand the need for separation of languages and language equity is because this environment provides students with a network of resources, including the two language systems, that the children can freely access for learning. Furthermore, the choice to support language development as freedom is aligned with a Vygotskian understanding of child development and the interrelationship between language and cognition. Language development and conceptual development, while being distinct, come together in our need to make meaning of the world in which we live. The dual-language education model, in this historical period, was creating the kind of language and cognitive classroom learning environments that facilitated the possibilities of the child using both languages for their development.

As most scholars conceptualize individual freedom in the service of freedom for others and as central to the concept of development as freedom are that the process and outcomes that generate more freedoms. To speak about language development as freedom is not enough. This freedom is connected to other freedoms that we will address within the next two sections: professional development as a freedom and intellectual development as a freedom.

I have worked in different settings in dual-language education programs and, while the teachers' conviction of what the environment for learning ought to be was certainly a driving force in this situation, as previously stated, there was yet another salient characteristic of the school environment. The school environment permitted the teachers to hang on to the beliefs they stood for, and to examine them. Furthermore, it helped the teachers improve on their capabilities for working with bilingual children—it was the engagement of teachers in professional development as freedom. We will look at this next.

ACTIVITIES

1. Interview two or three bilingual-program coordinators. Ask them questions about where decisions about language allocation are made? What do they ask teachers to consider when they are making decisions about allocating language for instruction? Is it based

on program model, on subject, on teachers, on children, etc.? What else do they consider? Ask the coordinator what teachers complain about and what amount of the professional development time is spent on talking about language distribution? Based on your findings, how would you compare them to what you read about in this chapter?

2. Attend a bilingual or dual-language teachers' meeting and notice what questions are asked. How would you frame the questions from the perspective of the relationships that you could see being negotiated? How would you rephrase the questions in terms of equity and/or social justice?

ENDNOTES

1. Olga Rubio is currently a professor in the Department of Teacher Education, College of Education, California State University, Long Beach.

2. Lemke, Jay L. "Articulating Communities: Sociocultural Perspectives on Science Education." *Journal of Research in Science Teaching,* 38 (2001): 296–316.

3. Id.

4. To support the outcomes of the first decision-making meeting, a series of staff development sessions ensued over a period of one year to unfold the new vision of the school. During the academic year, these program community gatherings became a forum for dialogue amongst dual-language teachers. A year later, the staff development extended to reach out to the monolingual teachers in the school. The colleague that worked with me at PS 165 the second year was Dr. James Purpura, a Teachers College colleague in Teaching English as a Second Language (TESOL). Our focus was on "English as a second language" methodologies. Throughout, we kept minutes and field notes of the meetings.

5. Cole, Michael. "Cognitive Development and Formal Schooling: The Evidence from Cross-cultural Research," in Luis Moll (ed.), *Vygotsky and Education: Instructional Implications and Applications of Sociohistorical Psychology.* (New York: Cambridge University Press, 1990, pp. 89–110).

6. From 1995 through 2002 Ron Unz, currently a software developer with Unz.org and who unsuccessfully ran for governor of California in 1994, was the sponsor for California Proposition 227 and launched an antibilingual education drive in the United States. In New York City he proposed a referendum to amend the city charter to eliminate bilingual education, but it never went very far. Nonetheless, the Department of Education subsequently limited the funding of bilingual education programs.

7. Cummins, James. "Empowering Minority Students: A Framework for Intervention. *Harvard Education Review,* 56 (1986): 18–36.

8. Skutnabb-Kangas, Tove, Ofelia Garcia, and María Torres-Guzmán, eds. *Imagining Multilingual Schools: Language in Education and Globalization.* (Philadelphia: Multilingual Matters, 2006).

9.   Amrein, Audrey, and Robert A. Peña. "Asymmetry in Dual-language Practice: Assessing Imbalance in a Program Promoting Equality." *EPAA,* 8 (2000) Available at http://epaa.asu.edu/epaa/v8n8.html. Last accessed March 2009.

10.   Since I worked closely with Ruth, people in the school district called me to ask what she meant and to express political concerns about the position of the native language vis-à-vis English.

11.   Garcia, Ofelia. "Lost in Transculturation: The Case of Bilingual Education in New York City" in Martin Pütz, Joshua A. Fishman, and Neff-Van Aertselaer (Eds.), *Along the Routes to Power: Exploration of the Empowerment through Language.* (Berlin: Mouton de Gruyter, 2006). pp. 157–178.

12.   Freeman, Rebecca. *Building on Community Bilingualism.* (Philadelphia: Caslon Publishing, 2004); Perez, Bertha. *Biliteracy Development.* (Mahwah, NJ: Lawrence Erlbaum, 2004).

13.   Machado, Antonio. *Campos de Castilla.* (Madrid, España: Editorial Alianza, 2006).

14.   Greene, Maxine. *Dialectics of Freedom.* (New York: Teachers College Press, 1988).

15.   See Malavet, Guillermo. *Hispanic Parents: Sociocultural Perspective on Family, Ideology, and Identity.* Doctoral dissertation, University of Arizona, 2006.

16.   Crawford, James. *At War with Diversity: U.S. Language Policy in an Age of Anxiety.* (Clevedon, UK: Multilingual Matters, 2000).

17.   Bialystok, Ellen, *Bilingualism in Development: Language, Literacy, & Cognition.* (New York: Cambridge University Press, 2001).

PART TWO

PROFESSIONAL DEVELOPMENT
AS FREEDOM

4

THE PROFESSIONAL
DEVELOPMENT PLAN

⤇

Prior to our relationship at PS 165, Ruth and I had focused on building a relationship of trust and developing a common vision on the
education of bilingual learners. Professional development was one of
the threads of conversation that we deepened at PS 165. We discussed
ways in which our joint work could help meet the needs of teachers.
There was a shortage of teachers grounded in theoretical knowledge
about language development and second-language acquisition and we
were both invested in increasing this pool of teachers.

We saw a university-school collaboration as benefiting each side greatly.
I had worked in Lansing, Michigan, with one of the first Holmes Professional Development Schools in the country. When I arrived at Teachers
College (TC), the establishment of a similar partnership was on the table.
The TC initiative culminated in the selection of the school district within
which Ruth worked. The specific participant schools selected, however,
I felt, were not the optimum settings for placing our bilingual teacher
education students. The number of bilingual preservice students was small
and there were many options for student teacher placement. I wanted
them to be in the dual-language education programs within the school
district because it had the first dual-language education program in the

city and exposure to it would give the future teachers a set of positive experiences from which to draw. Besides being in a bilingual classroom, we wanted the student-teaching placements to meet two other criteria. The placement had to have a significant number of students who were at various stages of bilingualism that would reflect linguistically and socially what schools were facing nationwide and the placements had to provide the student teachers with room to experiment with different ways of thinking about teaching. Given that we emphasized reflective teaching within our teacher education program, we wanted placements in which our students could expand and take on leadership roles in exploring teaching, in exploring the instructional language policies and practices they learned about at the university, and in whetting their appetite for extending this leadership role in teaching beyond the program and school levels.

Within PS 165, all of the teacher education program's expectations were possibilities as Ruth and I began our collaboration. We placed three student teachers during Ruth's first year as principal, and she hired them the second year. Having our former students as a cadre of teachers within the school facilitated developing a cohesive vision within the school about the need for reflective teaching. As Dewey[1] proposed, it is not just the experience, but the attentive consideration and meditation about the meaning of our experiences that constitute learning. Within their program of study, they had been exposed to reflective teaching practices. PS 165 was an opportunity for continuing to understand the value and study-in-practice of such teaching.

Before going to work with these three teachers, which we will come back to in the next chapter, I return to Ruth. She believed in the value of reflective teaching. How she set up the supervision of teachers and governance during her first year mirrored some of the same directions that I was proposing in other areas of teacher work.

Professional development, within, is proposed as the expansion of the network of resources (material and human) available to facilitate the teachers' need to find new ways of being teachers and learners. The collective structures were important for anchoring individual freedom. It was not a free-for-all, as there was direct or indirect intervention in what individual teachers did. Nonetheless, the contexts created were such that the teachers could personally choose to realize their individual freedom within the social groups[2] to which they related. This chapter will focus on describing the individual and collective structures set up by Ruth within the supervision and governance structures.

ENCOURAGING AUTONOMY AND RISK TAKING

Ruth recognized traditional supervision as a space of contention. Evaluations, and subsequent decisions, could have an impact on the life of the individual and his or her future employment. Something had to be different if Ruth were to improve teaching at the school. "Clinical observations," Ruth stated, "[were] too restrictive and limiting as learning experiences for the teachers." So, she began to experiment with a model of supervision that would integrate the needs of a changing school while ensuring teacher growth. Her idea of a supervision model was to create an environment that encouraged teacher autonomy and risk taking. She chose two activities that would involve her directly in the assessment and evaluation of a teacher's work while providing him or her with assistance in individual development—the portfolios and the curriculum conversations.

Portfolios

The teachers' union had just begun to promote teacher portfolios. A principal could base his or her evaluation on classroom observation or on teacher portfolios. Ruth seized this opportunity and gave the teachers the option of doing portfolios. The exception was the novice teacher. Ruth felt that the new teacher needed more direction and she did not feel the option of the portfolio was appropriate. She wanted to observe them while teaching. Initially, only seven teachers took up the teacher portfolio option, but by the end of Ruth's tenure only two teachers preferred the clinical supervision. This was evidence of the development of the teachers.

The experienced teacher, thus, could define his or her portfolio focus (later it could be a group project) and submit the portfolio for the principal's approval. The teachers had to define a question they wanted to work on throughout the year. They had to identify the methods for collecting the information. They were to submit their written proposals at the beginning of the year. A criterion for approval of a portfolio was that it be framed as teacher learning. The teachers had to show an ability to be accountable for their own professional development. At the end of the year, they had to submit a written (or multimedia) report explaining what they learned about the topic and about "self as educator."

Many of the portfolios took the form of teacher research. I, and a group of doctoral students, helped three graduates from the teacher education program to focus their questions, to discuss the appropriateness of methods for data gathering and data analysis, to provide supporting literature and resources, and to organize their reports. The range of topics of the portfolios during Ruth's tenure varied, but the dual foci of improvement of learning/instruction and reflection on their teaching practices were always present.

The portfolio was a way of promoting teacher professionalism and creating teacher autonomy. Teacher agency was a possibility, as the teachers were responsible and accountable for their own learning. The teachers could use their portfolios to document their reflective practices and their new ways of thinking and working. They could take on roles as creators, thinkers, curriculum developers, and problem solvers in their yearlong inquiries.

The portfolios triggered professional development in a dynamic way. Some of the teachers worked on themes such as (1) classroom management, (2) understanding how to develop reading skills, and (3) implementing a standard-based curriculum in the classroom.

Teams of teachers also created portfolios. For example, two teachers in the dual-language education fourth-grade class teamed up to develop a joint portfolio based on their detailed research on transferring from one language to the other. The team eventually coordinated their everyday schedules based on the information they gathered. The sharing of their ways of coordinating the team eventually took hold programwide.

During this period, the portfolios were also an impetus for whole school change. For example, a team of third-grade teachers collaborated on a portfolio that focused on aligning the English language standards with report cards in their assessment of the students. This work produced new report cards (in both languages) for the grade, and after they presented their research to the entire staff, it spearheaded a change in the report cards for the entire school. The change in report cards not only shifted the school's accountability relationship with parents, but it pushed teachers to reflect on ways to connect to the school and the community. They wanted the parents to be able to understand how schools assessed their children's progress and how they could think about helping their children or assess the assessment of their children's progress.

In addition to reporting on inquiries, the portfolios, more importantly, became a vehicle for displaying the new knowledge the teachers gained and created. For example, two second-grade, dual-language education teachers focused on transference skills in reading from Spanish to English. The teachers already knew the theories of transfer between first and second language, as expressed in Cummins's threshold hypothesis.[3] They knew that a strong foundation in the first language was necessary for both the transfer to the second language and academic success to be possible. They wanted to explore those cases where the theory did not easily explain what they were seeing in their classrooms. They decided to design a comparative case of bilingual language development. One of the teachers[4] wrote the following:

> I attempted to clarify what I referred to as the "neatness" theory of second language learning. This theory suggests that language develops at the same rate and in the same way for all children. I found it important to clarify this misconception for it can be detrimental to children who do not fit a neat model. For this reason, I chose to look at three children who demonstrated different language proficiencies and different points in their transferring of skills between languages. Their profiles illustrated that although general patterns of language transfers exist, each child reflected a unique language experience. Furthermore, this study recognized and clarified that language transfers do not only occur in a one-way direction. If there is a high level of comprehensible input in both languages' curriculum, children will transfer language skills from and to both languages.

This teacher portfolio is representative of the type of work teachers researched. The teachers did not propose to prove or disprove a theory. How they saw their task was to learn from a systematic exploration of a question in practice. The second-grade team wanted to understand how to approach a child with a variety of possible dispositions toward different languages.

The teacher team observed three students throughout the year. The students represented a theoretically based linguistic spectrum. They chose a model child who had a strong foundation in the first language and was moving into the second language seamlessly, as the theory proposes. The second child had a strong foundation in the native language but was having problems transferring to the second language. The third child had made the transfer to the second language and was showing signs of rejecting his first language.

The school's computer and technology specialist joined the team. His initial purpose was to support the team by videotaping reading events. The team gained greater understanding about the children, their book choices, their writing, and the transferability issues. The computer specialist learned from the team about second-language learning and subsequently developed new strategies for introducing computers to students who did not have strong language proficiencies in English.

Curriculum Conversations

Ruth transformed curriculum conversations into supervisory activities. She spoke about them as "accountable talk."[5] Ruth and each individual teacher would sit down for three conversations in the academic year. The conversations focused on student progress.

At the beginning of each year, Ruth asked the teachers to prepare an individual statement indicating their reading and writing philosophy, their major plans for the year, and the instructional plans for each of the students in their classroom. Each teacher was expected to discuss his or her goals and expectations for the whole class, for individual students, and his or her personal goals for professional growth during his or her first meeting with Ruth.

When the teachers unveiled their annual plans, they were expected to speak specifically to their commitment to developing skills and strategies appropriate for the grade level they taught. They also had to determine and articulate what they needed to accomplish in their classrooms and through their professional goals. As Ruth put it, she was committed to freeing the teachers from obstacles, limits, and constraints that would cause them to deviate from their commitment and promise so that at the end of the year there would be no "Oh, I couldn't achieve because … " victim statements.

Ruth stood in the space of believing that teachers were well meaning and capable of doing their best. She created trust and facilitated the teachers' questioning and creating alternatives to the problems they identified and the class and individual goals they established. And she put in place what would support the teachers so that they were acting in an environment of what Nussbaum[6] would call "combined capability" where both the individual and the environmental material, policy, and other forms of support existed.

The significant change in supervision was that now the teacher had to conceptualize him- or herself as part of the assessment process for improving instruction. Moreover, the teacher's responsibility and accountability for children's performance in the language and content was realized in the interaction between the teacher and the administration. It was a negotiated social contract.

The second conversation centered on the individual progress of each child. Samples of students' written work were used to determine the progress they were making. Through this conversation, Ruth gauged how teachers were relating to their students, how they were planning for the individual needs of their students, and most importantly, how the students' literacy was developing. The latter, she believed, was imperative to systematically gauge in order to move the school out of the SURR status. Ruth also explored each teacher's beliefs about the children in this conversation. She could determine if the teacher believed that the children were or were not deserving of the best education schools could offer. In general, the conversations gave Ruth an opportunity to assess the professional development in which the teachers were engaged. It also made visible to the teachers where they needed to improve their teaching practices, what supports had not been anticipated that needed to be put in place, and how the literacy initiatives were being integrated (or not) in all content areas.

The third, and last conversation, was where they reflected together on the year's work. The teachers had an opportunity to review how they had helped each student to achieve his or her academic and language goals. The students' performances on the annual language proficiency tests were available during the third conversation. It was one of the ways they assessed bilingual students' progress. It also provided an op-portunity for both Ruth and the teachers to address issues that needed changing and to set the course for planning during the summer. One of the teachers spoke to what this kind of conversation meant to her. She stated:

We had a meeting at the beginning of the year to assess where the kids were at. We had a conversation about individual needs, and then I shared with the administration what my goals and my ideas were on how I wanted to structure my curriculum to address the needs of the students. Having that conversation with them was very helpful, because they shared their own experiences on how they would do certain things. So, they provided that support at the beginning of the year and we just had a meeting this past, maybe like a month ago, where we discussed some of the things that we had established as goals that I wanted to accomplish for the year. They were very impressed with some of the improvements that my kids were making.

These new forms of supervision had the effect of strengthening the teachers' commitment to the school. It also changed the relationships between the principal and teachers in the school. Teachers were more willing to take instructional risks while shifting the power hierarchy from principal-teacher to colleagues. They had jointly established common objectives. With respect to the ongoing conversation that it created between the teachers and the principal, this is what one of the teachers told us:

> I brought every piece of work that I did in my classroom to the principal. I would go in and say, "See what amazing work I did today. Here it is." I was at the back of the classroom and did *a, b,* and *d.* What amazing work.... You have to show your philosophy. I would come in and tell the principal, "I teach skills. I do this. I read the whole guidebook, but I am not going to need it. I took out all the skills that are there. You want me to teach skills, this is how I am going to teach them. I am going to do it this way." Just like that. She was great because she didn't necessarily want people using the book this way; she wants teachers to have an understanding of them [the content and the skills]. I did not understand that my first year. I thought it ran contrary to all my beliefs.

The conversations were instrumental in developing close professional ties and they permitted Ruth to explore the strengths of her teachers. She told me that this permitted her to move them into positions where they could be assets to the school, while decreasing union grievances. Teacher development was the result of engaging in nontraditional roles, of openly conversing about the difficulties of teaching children in two languages, and of promoting risk taking and teacher autonomy.

COLLABORATIVE LEADERSHIP AND GOVERNANCE

Complex learning organizations, like PS 165, with an increasingly diverse student population, call for different kinds of leadership than in the past. In addition to being a principal with a moral imperative, Ruth saw that PS 165 needed to broaden its leadership.[7] As previously stated, Ruth established both a value-driven and collaborative leadership that respected children, their languages, and their cultures, and where language equity and the protection of the minoritized language were explicit norms. The leadership she established was inclusive of others. Ruth facilitated and expanded spheres of influence and participation. The school community—that is, parents and community members as well as teachers from regular education and other programs—were active participants in a variety of school initiatives. The end-of-the year retreat was one of the school structures that best illustrated how the expanded leadership created spaces of freedom for participation for all involved.

At the end-of-the-year retreats, the school community established priorities for the coming year and revisited the previous year's rules of governance. The retreat was important because it broadened the support for shifts during the upcoming year. The school community examined teaching and learning, the role of teachers, and the relationship of the school with the community. The Schoolwide Project Committee (also known as the School Leadership Team, SLT) was the basic structure for governance in the school, and its members—teachers, parents, support staff, and administration—were the ones who planned the annual event in the spirit of collectively examining the annual progress of the school. The SLT Ruth had encountered when she arrived was skeletal, at best. To strengthen it, Ruth provided participating teachers additional preparation time during the school day so that they could attend meetings at convenient times for parents. The objective was doing away with barriers and creating conditions for greater communication between the school and the community.

The retreats usually occurred in the school building during the day in the month of May to ensure that all staff and parents who were willing to participate could do so. Principal, parents, and teachers organized the agenda collaboratively to ensure that the different concerns of different constituents that emerged during the year became part of the dialogue. Ruth saw her role as working to ensure that there were clear parameters within which the group worked and that the integrity of decisions made during the retreat were upheld during the year.

The decision-making process was highly participatory and open. Consensus was important and Ruth saw her role as probing intentions and anticipating outcomes. Her intention was to try to foresee and hedge potential conflicts with the basic philosophy of the school. Ruth would annually repeat her stance for inclusion of linguistic and cultural differences in the form of a 50/50 dual-language program, while opening the discussion on methods for reaching the goals of language equity and minoritized language preservation. Engaging in a values-driven leadership[8] and ensuring that the process was open and participatory and inclusive of the different constituents enabled Ruth to work as an inspiring leader. She leveled the playing fields and then sought new ways of working to ensure the organizational, personal, and professional development of those involved.

There were two half-days in May dedicated to the retreat. On the first day, school personnel and community members assessed the progress of the different programs in the school. On the second day, they made plans for the following school year based on the information they had processed the first day. Decisions made at the retreat, in terms of school organization and structure, were implemented during the following year. The integrity of the decisions was in question at all times. Ruth knew this and was keen to possible dissension that might be associated with sole decisions she had to make. This did not stop her from making decisions, even if they were hard ones to make. She had a bottom line and she was the ultimate decision maker. Within the retreat structure, however, once the decisions were made, they were generally accepted, embraced, and enacted. The spirit of trust, value, and ethics-based decisions from the retreat helped inspire the schoolwide transformation. The school became an institution that examined itself. A structure of decision making was implemented with a range of tolerance and flexibility that could accommodate the shifts during the year without impairing, in any significant way, the vision established at the end of the year.

Engaging more people in leadership feeds on the social value of democracy. It also provided the school personnel and community a sense of participation, not only because they belonged to a community but also because they wanted to make a difference in their world. PS 165 transformed their decision-making process into shared governance. Sharing in the leadership of a school often brings greater diversity of thinking and thus could lead to opening social spaces and possibilities for better addressing the diverse needs of the children the school serves. We have seen many reforms, like decentralization, community schools, community-based management, just to name a few, that purport to democratize school decision making. What happened in PS 165 was different in two ways. Similar to what Quintero[9] described in her book, *Muchas Reformas, Pocos Cambios* [Many Reforms, Few Changes], many aspects of the organization had to be tackled at once. This ensured transformation of ways in which people related to each other and to their students and school community; it was more than a surface change. The essence of how an individual learns and the role of language in the learning and communication of the learning were key to the new ways of thinking and acting at PS 165. Second, the shared leadership was not a response to external communities mandating a role in school decisions, nor did it come from any mandate from above. Collaborative leadership came from a convergence of sorts. Coming together were a community placing hope in the school, a group of teachers wanting to improve their student's performance, a school threatened with closure by the state, and an inspirational principal who understood her moral mandate with respect to the culturally and linguistically diverse student population of the school.

Within, I have described the end-of-the-year retreat as an example of how collaborative leadership came to be at PS 165. The new ways of conducting business in the school stimulated instructional and curriculum dialogue in the school and communitywide. This further moved the teachers to break their isolation and go beyond their classrooms, their programs, and their school conversations, as we will see in the following two chapters.

ACTIVITIES

1. If you were to create a teaching portfolio that would focus on your development as a teacher, what do you think you would include? Develop the front matter of your portfolio. How would you communicate to your readers what they ought to focus on—your purpose? How would you break it up (by subjects, by strengths and subjects, by your learning within the subject areas, etc.)? How would you communicate the criteria you used to select the different materials presented in the portfolio? How do you communicate the everyday learning in your classroom? How do you communicate what learning occurs over time? How do you make the presentation multidimensional? What kind of media would you use?

2. Interview the local school principal where there is either a large number of children who are learning English as a second language or where there is a program of bilingual education established. Find out how they make decisions about the teachers' professional development and the role the teachers play in participating in those decisions. Find out how the principal supervises the teachers and what criteria he or she uses.

ENDNOTES

1. Dewey, John. *Democracy and Education: An Introduction to the Philosophy of Education.* (New York: The Free Press, 1944).

2. Greene, Maxine. *Dialectics of Freedom.* (New York: Teachers College Press, 1988).

3. Cummins, James. "Linguistic Interdependence and the Educational Development of Bilingual Children." *Review of Educational Research,* 2 (1979): 222-251.

4. Arana, B. Reflection from the Inside. Unpublished Dissertation. Teachers College Columbia University (2004), p. 114.

5. Resnick, Lauren B., Clotilde Pontecorvo, and Roger Säljö, eds. *Discourse Tools and Reasoning: Essays on Situated Cognition.* (New York: Springer, 1997).

6. Nussbaum, Martha. *Women and Human Development.* (Cambridge, UK: Cambridge University Press, 2000).

7. Fullan, Michael. *The Moral Imperative of School Leadership.* (Thousand Oaks, CA: Corwin Press, 2003); Senge, Peter. *The Fifth Discipline: The Art and Practice of the Learning Organization.* (New York: Doubleday Currency, 1990).

8. Gold, A., J. Evans, P. Earley, D. Halpin, and P. Callarbone. "Principled Principals? Values-driven Leadership: Evidence from Ten Case Studies of 'Outstanding' School Leaders." *Educational Management & Administration,* 31 (2003): 127–138.

9. Quintero, Ana Helvia. *Muchas Reformas Pocos Cambios: Hacia Otras Metáforas Educativas.* (Hato Rey, Puerto Rico: Publicaciones Puertorriqueñas, 2006).

5

THE MANY BENEFITS OF GROUP STUDY

In many of the collaborative teacher structures, the teachers experienced themselves as learners, as experts, and as leaders. In addition to the team teaching mentioned previously, they came together in grade-level teams, in meetings across programs, and across grades through looping and through study groups. Each of these forms had their purpose. One of the teachers commented as follows about the basic collaboration—grade-level teams:

> The grade team—we have a common prep every Monday. We all meet; we try to help each other out and give each other ideas of activities. Our level teachers work very well with Mr. X.... Two teachers in special education join us. Mrs. M and I are partners. We go on all the trips during the year together. We work on special activities in the school. Our level teachers are close. You are leaders. Be it emotional, with materials, whatever. That is what I like about what is occurring now. Years ago, we did not have a common time to prepare.

The varied types of professional development were important in creating an ethos of collaboration that was still part of the school's reputation many years after Ruth's retirement. Within this chapter, however, I will focus on the professional development practices that focused on study and inquiry. I will describe two foundational groups: the Classroom Ethnography Study Group that took place in Ruth's second year of tenure at PS 165 and the Reading Book Club that took place in Ruth's third year as principal. Subsequently, I will focus on two structures that evolved and Ruth left in place when she retired—the Professional Development School Partnership and the teacher study groups. Since there were close to 17 study groups at the time Ruth retired and would require a book in itself to describe, I will highlight the work of just one: the Dual-Language Study Group, which is most directly relevant to the special issues of culture, language, teaching/learning, and freedom.

CLASSROOM ETHNOGRAPHY STUDY GROUP

The Classroom Ethnography Study Group was the initial study group. It began in 1993, during Ruth's second year as principal. She invited me to start working with the teachers at the school, and I had expressed my desire to focus on teacher reflection as a way of understanding what the experience of teachers working in bilingual settings could reveal to us about working with bilingual children. Ruth had hired three of my former master's degree students and she asked me to start with them. They knew about reflection. They had completed what we call the master's integrative project, in which they used their student teaching/teaching practices as a space for inquiry. In addition, they had expressed a desire to continue exploring the relationships between theory and practice in their classrooms.

I approached the three former students and they agreed to work with me. I brought in a group of bilingual doctoral students and with the three teachers we created a space for conversation and reflection about teaching in a dual-language setting. The doctoral students and I would observe classrooms. The teachers determined our focus, and we would share our written descriptions in field notes with them.[1] In other words, the external observers would focus on an internally derived area of study. Our outside perspective would inform their concerns and curiosities about their own teaching inquiries.

We observed weekly, but met all together as a study group once a month. In the monthly meetings, we discussed classroom social interactions and social organizations observed. We had a joint discussion, and this gave the teachers an opportunity to react, reflect, and respond. Through the ongoing interactions, the university group and school personnel began shifting their relationship, tearing at the barriers that separated us, both because of the vestiges from prior relationships and because of the traditional notions embodied in the researcher/teacher relationship. As time passed, the teachers assumed more power and agency within the relationship.

At the end of the first year of our work, they reflected on what they had learned through this experience about themselves. Their reflections were presented in the form of a teacher portfolio. One of the teachers focused on math and language. Math was a subject that constituted one of her teaching discomforts, and she was concerned that she did not provide the children what they needed in this subject. Another teacher explored the writing process in two languages, as he was unclear on how to organize the writing. He felt that the daily switching of languages was somewhat antithetical to the development of a cohesive unit in writing. The children would either have two writing exercises going on, or the switching would have to occur after each unit. The third teacher was concerned with organizing the classroom for learning, assuming classroom authority still clashed with some of her internalized views of what classrooms should be like.

Making teaching problems their own—rather than the system's, the administrators', or the parents'—was critical to the teachers' inquiry. They problematized the issues of teaching by focusing on their individual aspects of wonderment. They were nervous about other adults observing them, as one of the teachers wrote:

> At first I found myself performing for them, trying to be the sort of Platonic form of "teacher" that I have in the back of my mind. Considering my inexperience, this may have been slightly comical (or painful?) to watch. It didn't take long for me to forget they were there—I am much too busy in the classroom acting and reacting to be too concerned that someone might think I'm a lousy teacher.

The group provided these three teachers a way of finding solutions that freed them from the past weighty isolation and burden they carried on their own. It enabled the teachers to be within the problems in ways they had not felt possible previously. It was within the group that one of the teachers expressed having found personal and professional freedom, as she now understood why she felt insecure about math.

The work of the group was also important because it created new forms of teacher leadership within the school.[2] As these teachers began to talk to their colleagues about their projects, interest grew. Eventually, study groups would emerge as the strongest way of doing professional development.

The purpose of inquiry was to engage in epistemological curiosity—systematically reflecting on both the theory and practice of a curricular, programmatic, or instructional theme.[3] In the study groups, teachers shared with each other teaching experiences and student work, pondered difficult questions, and began establishing "norms of continuous learning."[4] In addition to creating intellectual interest among others in the school about this new way of thinking about teacher development, their specific inquiries helped them develop the kind of understanding they needed about learning and teaching that would help the non-English-speaking student population to develop academically. This reconceptualization of teaching led to a view of teaching "as professional problem solving."[5] The inquiry groups were more like individuals supporting each other in teacher research, in their classrooms similar to the ethnographic study group. I will describe a study group with a bit more of the complexity of doing this work, but before doing so, I will describe an early group that was a precursor to more schoolwide teacher collaborative activity.

THE READING GROUP

Ruth and eight teachers began a fiction-reading club a year after the classroom ethnography study group formed. The Reading Book Club met once a month for two years (1995–1997) at the house of a teacher who lived two blocks from the school. The group decided to create a social and nonthreatening atmosphere with snacks, wine, and dinner. Members of the group explored their own experiences as readers as they analyzed and discovered new insights in the literature books they read. Weaving the pleasure of reading with intense analysis of the texts gave the group new understanding about reading. Reading became more than a set of skills; the teachers began to realize that meaning did not solely come from the text. They brought to a more conscious level the fact that it was a combination of the author, the reader with his or her prior knowledge, and the context of the reading that brought meaning to the text.[6] The knowledge about reading, gained from the process of self-awareness, did not stop there. At a later point, the teachers moved to consciously translate and transform what they had learned in the reading group into classroom practices that helped children. Teachers thus developed fundamentally new ways of working to improve school literacies in their classrooms and these served to promote higher level thinking skills among students. This group contributed significantly to changes in relationships between Ruth and the teachers; it was here where they created an environment conducive to becoming a learning community. The Reading Group was a basis for bringing the Teachers College Reading and Writing Project into the school down the road.

TEACHER INQUIRY/STUDY GROUP

I have conflated two types of groups because they started as one and then separated, but at times they merged, depending on the administrative support and the needs of the school's teachers. The teacher study groups are explicit before- or after-school meetings of teachers, where they engage in dialogue and review research about instruction and curriculum. Inquiry groups are social spaces where teachers talk about their concerns, wonderings, and curiosities. It is where they systematically do inquiry on a topic.

In the PS 165 teacher study groups, the topics were determined early in the school year. Since the topic had been predetermined in a broad sense, there was a process of narrowing that occurred over time and was explicitly discussed at the end of each of the meetings. One of the members would volunteer to select, organize, and distribute readings, and to lead the next meeting discussion. The teachers in the group came to each meeting ready to share reflections about their understanding of the reading and to identify and describe practices they engaged in that would connect with the readings. Questions would also be formulated for the group to explore. In these physical and social spaces, the teachers would test their interpretations in relation to those of others. In this setting, they shared their positive experiences and their worries, their problems, and their discomforts. They went from thought into action as they shared material and methods. The teachers bonded and helped each other, breaking the common model of the traditional teacher in an isolated classroom. Teachers gained the confidence and courage to try new methods, lessons, or just ways of being in their classrooms. It was, perhaps, the space where the school's ethos of collaboration was most fully expressed.

Although led by administration or university personnel in their initial stages, the study groups evolved to be teacher initiated and led. I came to understand the study group as embodying the cultural ways of the school during Ruth's tenure. It was a place where teachers affirmed collective and individual ways of thinking, acting, and being.

By the time Ruth retired, teachers began to see the study group as a structure for professional accountability. A year prior to Ruth's retirement, one of the bilingual teachers invited other teachers to create a new opportunity to reflect on the development and implementation of successful literacy practices across grades and programs. The consensus was that the study groups were vehicles for pedagogical accountability. They wanted to break with the traditional hierarchical forms of accountability, that is, accountability solely to the principal of the school. Winds were whispering about Ruth's possible retirement. Thus, the teachers initiated study groups and secured administrative support for substitutes so that they could visit each other's classrooms, provide coaching, and engage in other community learning activities. They created a strong teacher community that could withstand the impending administrative changes. They were trying to ensure, in light of a leadership change, that they as teachers would maintain a certain degree of power over that for which they were responsible—the curriculum and instruction.

In Ruth's last year, there was a surge in the number of study groups, culminating in 17 distinct groups. The following is the story of one of the groups—the Dual-Language Study Group—which emerged upon Ruth's retirement. It illustrates the kind of work teachers can accomplish.

DUAL-LANGUAGE STUDY GROUP[7]

After a few years experiencing some success, the dual-language teachers began noticing a lull when Ruth retired. There had been a communication gap growing between the lower- and upper-grade dual-language teachers. The teachers decided to meet regularly. The change in administration, the modifications of curriculum schoolwide with the new math programs, and TC reading and writing workshop process for teaching literacy called for stock taking and renewal. The teachers within the dual-language program were participating unevenly in these new projects and they found themselves loosing common ground across the grades. One of the dual-language teachers, Berta Alvarez, and one of the teachers participating in the Professional Development School (PDS) partnership, Ms. Rebecca Madrigal, proposed a Dual-Language Study Group. In a national presentation, Rebecca told the following story.

The first step of the group was to brainstorm the topics they wanted to discuss. They wanted to articulate the vision and mission that would guide them through the upcoming administrations—many, as it turned out. The group's goal was to improve the program and deal with the growing academic gap between the lower and upper grades. The teachers were released during regular school hours and they were provided remuneration for their extra work, time, and effort, when it was possible. They were realistic about the fact that new administrations might not be as generous. Thus, the teachers set their meeting time to Tuesdays at 7:30 a.m. twice a month before school hours. Most of the teachers were willing participants and attended the meetings.

The new feature of the Dual-Language Study Group was that it was teacher led. The first year, the group decided not to have an agenda to follow or a specific inquiry on which to focus. The year was an opportunity to explore freely a variety of topics, ideas, meeting structures, goals, concerns, and future inquiries. The time they took to explore solidified their role as advocates for the children they served.[8] Madrigal wrote:

> I considered it [the first year] to be the beginning of a dynasty of teachers who wanted to be heard and who wanted to impact their students' learning. Each teacher opened his/her mind and heart to make possible that we could feel the honesty with which we tackled the issues.

There were plenty of topics on the list. It gave the teachers a realistic sense of what the present and the future would be. They could not see their work as calling for a quick fix; it would be ongoing. In addition, there were the passions and tensions involved in different aspects of their work. Madrigal writes: "As we contemplated the list, we also became present to the reality that this was a red flag— we had a long road ahead and working collaboratively was imperative."

Discussion, prioritizing, and new discussions led to ten topics that were subsequently divided into four components. The first was around the Spanish component of the program and the Spanish materials. The second was on the support for new teachers and new teams and the across grade issues. The third was on revisiting the vision and the mission, on how the program was viewed by people outside the program within the school and among parents and visitors. They were specifically concerned about the promotional literature, about the constant visits to their school, and about a group of parents who were requesting monolingual educational settings. The last issue was on sustaining the group on a voluntary basis and continuing to command administrative support.

After mulling over the topics, the teachers narrowed them to two: the variations of Spanish and the standardization of Spanish terminology across the grades and making the program visible to the public.

At the beginning, the organization of the group depended on the topic. For example, when the Spanish component decided to take on language diversity and academic language as an issue, the large group split into two smaller groups. The Spanish component teachers developed a nonfiction reading unit with a focus on language standardization, while the English component teachers focused on promoting the program throughout the community by creating a pamphlet for it. The group as a whole chose the structures, topics, and activities. In order to accommodate the topic needs, they had to alternate the meetings. The first month the small groups met and the next month they would meet as a whole group to report on the subgroup's progress and to share and critique their work.

I turn to the Spanish component because it deals with a component of language that many bilingual teachers face—language variation and standardization. The teachers arrived at this topic because they agreed that their students knew certain literacy concepts but that they did not have a consistent academic vocabulary. Many of them also converged in their observations that the disconnect students experienced with the school language was exacerbated during their transitions from one school year to the next. The study group members proposed that inconsistency in their use of academic terminology might be related. If they provided consistency, the students might find themselves on a stronger footing to negotiate available synonyms or phrases in the different linguistic variations in Spanish. This consistency in the academic language would, in turn, solidify the students' academic vocabulary and deal with the gap between grades.

The linguistic variation of talk in the classroom stemmed, in part, from the richness and diversity in the language and cultural backgrounds of the teaching staff. Madrigal wrote:

> We felt that our national, cultural, and thus representational diversity promoted positive role models for the students and the community. It also helped the students, who themselves were from different backgrounds, to negotiate the different varieties they brought to the classroom.

The other side of this richness were the difficulties that emerged when they had to translate the concepts. They received external professional development primarily in English. The teachers were left to translate all the components—delivery, conversations, and materials—into the realities of the non-English classroom language use. One of the constraints the Spanish component teachers faced was that in addition to implementing what they learned, they had to translate, modify, and adapt it all to the reality of their Spanish classrooms. They were up to the task and did what they needed to do. It was here that they identified a significant problem. Within the individual translations, the linguistically and culturally rich teaching staff translated into a variety of Spanish standards—from Cuba, El Salvador, Ecuador, the Dominican Republic, Puerto Rico, and Mexico. When the group thought deeply about this kind of linguistic diversity in their program, they decided to test their assertion about the problem in a very concrete way. They felt they had to test how developing a group standard for academic language might connect favorably with the depth of students' academic language. Some of this understanding came from observing and listening to students. For example, Madrigal writes:

> We had common experiences with introducing certain concepts for writing and reading, where students did not react in expected ways. More than one of us had heard students comment, "*Sí nosotros sabemos como se llama esa característica. Pero la maestro, Ms. Serrano, le llamaba 'palabras en negrita' y no 'palabras remarcadas en negro*" ["We know what the characteristic is called, but Ms. Serrano calls it 'words in black' and not 'words highlighted in black'"]. Thus, we surmised that because we were creating our own individual terminology or using our own national standards, we were not using a standardized school terminology, and this was affecting children's academic progress, especially in literacy.

Given these connections, the teachers further grappled with their realization that the successful implementation of the new literacy approach with the Reading and Writing Project (TC) would require extra time and effort. The teachers would not only have to take time to do the usual adaptations and modifications that are required to take theory into practice, but they would also have to take time and effort to think about how the principles embedded in the curriculum applied to the children. Translations and standardization of the non-English academic language into Spanish would also be necessary. The thinking through of all these variables guided the inquiry group to focus on an intervention that they might test. They decided on developing a nonfiction reading unit. The objective of the exercise was to start a common Spanish academic standard language among the teachers that would ultimately benefit the students. There were very intensive conversations about how to decide on the appropriate Spanish terminology for this specific unit because each teacher felt very strongly about the terms that they were already using. However, these discussions helped to make the Spanish component teachers realize that they needed to work in collaborative ways that permitted them to use each other's expertise. Some of them would have to give up their words and phrases.

During the time the teachers were designing the nonfiction unit, they applied the unit in their classrooms. At each subsequent meeting, they shared their findings and considered ways to modifying the unit. Madrigal wrote:

> Our efforts were rewarded when we observed the students in the following grade; the teachers observed them to feel more confident with the vocabulary and the concepts.

The teachers had taken a long-term, collaborative view to their work. They were now ready to deepen the students' level of understanding by harnessing their own linguistic diversity in favor of an academic standard from which they could expand their own and students' academic vocabulary. The Dual-Language Study Group served as a strong leadership group advocating for and using their own problem-solving role in the matter of pushing students' thinking and learning with rigor.

SCHEDULES, TIME, AND ACCOUNTABILITY

"Time is a major issue, prep time is insufficient," one of the teachers said.[9] Preparation time, also called "prep," is a time within the school day in which the teachers can focus on planning, correcting papers, preparing instructional material, and the like. That is in theory. Most of the time, prep time is taken up by administrative duties.

At PS 165, the administration had to move beyond prep time to what they came to call "sacred" times. Sacred times were the time the school organized for team meetings, grade meetings, and across-grade meetings. In addition to the school-organized sacred times, the teachers set up meetings before and after school in order to attend study groups and complete their teacher portfolios. The distinction was that the before- or after-school teachers meetings and the sacred times were not absorbed by administrative issues. They were self-driven, mostly focused on curricular issues, although at times inclusive of mandated items. It was the teacher members of the team, the grade, the across-grade groups, and the study groups who determined the agendas, who determined and distributed the work, and who focused on the conversations that engaged them in considering the relationships between independence, interdependence, empowerment, and social justice.

The school schedule was organized to support these teacher needs. Teachers were provided substitute and cluster teachers so that they could, in turn, do professional development, mentoring, external workshops, and team and grade meetings, among other activities. The teachers had requested that the schedule accommodate their time for planning instructional and curricular activities, making decisions about new curricular programs and materials, and developing relationships with each other. The administration agreed with the teachers that their time had to be protected from disruptions from external programs. Thus, a broad view of what was occurring in the school was necessary. The administration needed to know who was overbooked and when new initiatives had to be postponed for the subsequent year. This was done through the schedule.

A good schedule, in their minds, was one that was open, visible, consistent yet flexible, and inclusive. It had to be visibly open. The teachers and administrators needed a schedule that did not hide anything, nor make anyone unknown—even free time ought to be scheduled, everything labeled, and everything demystified. The consistency of the schedule was important for the children as "it would upset children when there were any inconsistencies to their expected schedules."[10] And, simultaneously, the schedule had to be flexible, because even when it was considered finished, it had to be able to accommodate what would come up unexpectedly such as teacher illness or the like. Finally, the schedule had to be inclusive, for there had to be something for everyone or else it did not work.

The assistant principal talked extensively about the schedule in relation to providing teachers' free time and how to use the schedule to know when a teacher was so involved in activity that he or she did not attend to study and development. The freedom teachers were offered through the schedule flexibility was for learning. This was monitored. The assistant principal stated:

> Teachers need different spaces with regards to specific things. How do you do it so it makes sense? What do you give up? How can you finagle something so that everybody wins? I pretty much enjoy it ... moving

one spot to another. This teacher would take care of this, this one would take care of that. When it works, I feel really good about it. You bring in substitutes to help you work the schedule so that it makes sense. In terms of supporting teachers, you do so with money and with substitutes. It is not necessarily money for materials, but you pay someone else so you can free the teacher up. You support them and do not always make them give up prep. You find a space for them where you can get them out of something else so that they can come in and feel clear about what they have to do.

The schedule that I create has everyone in it. All you have to do is move one thing to another until you get what you want.... Free time is slotted in. Everything is slotted. You have your cluster teachers who you support plus your regular classroom teacher. So it's a matter of checking. So, she has the Philharmonic. So and so is covering her but she also has the Philharmonic here as her prep, so we have to cover her over here. I think that something that frees the schedule is the fact that it is an open schedule. Nothing is hidden. Every teacher and class has a code and has you totally demystify it, you just label the spaces with codes.... Then you have some things etched in stone, which are the priorities. Literacy, common preps are etched in stone.... Through the schedule you get to see what is not being done as well. Someone may have a lot of special programs. Well, you know that he is not leaving any time for study.

Having time to study, having time to think is part of the freedom teachers do not experience in many schools. It was this freedom that permitted teachers to think about the fundamental aspects of their profession and to contribute to each other's development. One of the teachers told me that the principal provided her the freedom to teach in ways that were more student oriented, but a new teacher spoke about her freedom in another way. She said she had requested a basal because she still did not know how to handle her freedom to determine what to do; the principal had permitted her to go in this direction with the explicit agreement that she would strive to become more independent and creative in her teaching. The teachers were not all in one space, but there was an ethos where teachers could disengage from the everyday events in schools and classrooms to distance themselves and reflect on their work.

In time, the meaning of accountability was also transformed. Most teachers believed evaluation and accountability was necessary, but they understood these concepts in a way that was different from the rhetoric of many policy makers. For example, by the end of Ruth's tenure the literacy study group came together to create "accountability" amongst the teachers. They anticipated the change in administration and decided to proactively organize themselves to establish collegial structures, much like the medical profession, to ensure that the teaching personnel established a standard amongst themselves. It was a way of establishing a standard of behavior to which the teaching personnel and the administration of the school would also be held.

Within this chapter, I have described the different structures of professional development at PS 165. I finished with some of the administrative items, such as time, schedules, and accountability that had to be transformed to support the teachers in inquiry. In the next chapter, I will describe the support structures—the freedoms and responsibilities—coming from the university/school partnership.

ACTIVITIES

1. Imagine you were part of a study group with a focus on the education of children who were not English proficient yet. You have to develop your own question about your work with this population. There is no question out of bounds. What would your question be?

2. Take an inquiry walk around a local school. Your questions are: What are ways of communicating that are visible to you at the local school? How does the school communicate with the parents and the outside school community? What is visible as you walk into the main office? When you enter the main office, what evidence is there that administrators and teachers are in daily communication? What evidence is there of teacher-student communication outside the classroom?

ENDNOTES

1. The observers wrote up their notes weekly and shared them with the teachers. We did not do videotaping as we felt it a bit intrusive to start out with. I had previously worked with an ethnographic study on teacher development at Michigan State University. For more information on the details of the latter project, see Campbell, D. "Collaboration and Contradiction in a Research and Staff Development Project." *Teachers College Record,* 90, 1 (1986): 99–121.

2. Lieberman, Ann. "Teacher Leadership." *Teachers College Record,* 88, 3 (1987): 400–425; Barthes, Roland. "Teacher Leader." *Phi Delta Kappan,* 82, 6 (2001): 443–449.

3. Freire, Paolo. *Pedagogy of Freedom: Ethics, Democracy, and Civic Courage.* (Lanham, MD: Rowman and Littlefield, 2001).

4. Trachtman, Roberta. *The NCATE Professional Development School Study: A Survey of 28 PDS Sites.* Unpublished manuscript, 1996. Available from Professional Development School Standards Project, National Council for Accreditation of Teachers Education, Washington, D.C., 20036.

5. Myers, Charles B. *Beyond PDSs: Schools as Professional Learning Communities. A Proposal Based on an Analysis of PDS Efforts of the 1990s.* Paper presented at annual meeting of the American Educational Research Association, New York (1996, April), as cited in Abdal-Haqq, I. Constructivism in Teacher Education: Consideration or those who would like practice to theory. (ERIC Clearinghouse on Teaching and Teacher Education, American Association of Colleges for Teacher Education Washington, D. C., 20515, 1998). Retrieved February 28, 2009, from http://www.ericdigests.org/1999-3/theory.htm.

6. Rosenblatt, Louise M. *The Reader, the Text, the Poem.* (Carbondale: Southern Illinois University Press, 1978); Barthes, Roland. *Image, Music, Text.* (Glasgow, UK: Collins Fontana, 1977); Harris, P., and J. Trezise. "Intertextuality and Beginning Reading Instruction in the Initial School Years." *Journal of Australian Research in Early Childhood Education,* 1 (1997): 32–39.

7. This section is based on Rebecca Madrigal's section of Torres-Guzmán, Maria E., Victoria Hunt, Ivonne M. Torres, Rebecca Madrigal, Isabel Fletcha, Stephanie Lukas, and Alcira Jaar. "Teacher Study Groups: In Search of Teaching Freedom." *The New Educator,* 2 (2006): 207–226.

8. Cummins, James. "The Role of Primary Language Development in Promoting Educational Success for Language Minority Students" in California State Department of Education, Office of Bilingual Bicultural Education, *Schooling and Language Minority Students: A Theoretical Framework.* (Los Angeles: California State University, Evaluation, Dissemination, and Assessment Center, 1981, pp. 3-50).

9. Aronowitz, Stanley, and Henry Giroux. *Education Under Siege: The Conservative, Liberal and Radical Debate over Schooling.* (New York: Routledge, 1987).

10. Interview with Interim Principal Evelyn Marzan, Transcript, March 1999.

6

THE SYNERGY OF COLLABORATION
TEACHERS AND RESEARCHERS TOGETHER

As mentioned previously, Ruth and I believed and worked towards creating a school/university relationship with concrete projects. My concern going into this relationship was a guarantee that our master's degree students would have placements in a school where experienced teachers would take on the role of mentoring new teachers into the teaching profession and where our students would have a space to experiment with methods generated from new pedagogical theories. To reciprocate, I agreed to engage faculty and doctoral students in providing the teachers of the school with support for their ongoing professional development.

In the previous chapters, I described the different forms of professional development that took place. In this chapter, I will describe how this partnership expanded. In addition, I highlight what a systematic look at the relationship meant for our teacher education students and for the teachers at PS 165 as we tried to break with traditional hierarchies and isolation. The overarching structure, the Teachers College Community School District #3 (TC/CSD#3) Professional Development School Partnership (PDS),[1] provided the opportunity for both expansion beyond the bilingual settings and the breaking of teacher isolation.

THE PROFESSIONAL DEVELOPMENT SCHOOL

The discussion about formalizing the partnership began three years into Ruth's tenure. By then, the school had been acknowledged locally as a transforming school and had acquired some national recognition for its dual-language education program. Its reputation of having a collaborative ethos was also reaching the teaching cohort seeking new environments in schools.

Ruth and I had a fluid, informal relationship. We knew that if the school took on the formal status of a PDS school, it could play a pivotal role in redesigning and improving both preservice and in-service teacher education.[2] A benefit for the school was the potential expansion of services available from the College's human and technical resources. PS 165 could influence the College's ability to educate teachers for inner-city schools with large minoritized language populations. For the relationship to continue to grow, it had to go beyond us. It had to be institutionalized.

By the time Naomi Hill, from the College's PDS Office, approached us about joining the PDS, we knew what we wanted. We took our shared vision to the negotiating table. I was interested in recognition of our teacher education program's past work, in having PDS bilingual interns, and in expanding the resources available to prepare teachers to work with minoritized language students. Ruth was keen on establishing internships in teaching and having a space at the table that would help the school deal with two issues: examining the relationship between the student teachers and their cooperating teachers and broadening the arena for teachers' professional growth and development.

I had multiple meetings with the teachers at which we discussed student teaching and PDS internships. I began to see the teachers' understandings about professional growth and development. They understood that while student teaching had the potential of being the most critical aspect of teacher development for an aspiring teacher, the traditional forms of student teaching did not adequately prepare the future teachers for the rigors of the job. This was a particularly valid assessment for those teachers who aspired to work in schools, like PS 165, where the students were poor, urban, and from the inner city where many were speakers of multiple languages.

The teachers had learned a few things on the job and they were willing to share these with new teachers-to-be. They could play a supportive role for those going through student teaching and the PDS internships. They felt they could bring something unique to the table—their knowledge about teaching language minorities in an inner-city school—and into TC courses by teaching as clinical faculty. This arrangement was exciting for PS 165 teachers.

The teachers were realistic about their skills, knowledge, and dispositions. They acknowledged themselves to be products of the traditional conceptualization and implementation of student teaching. They felt the experience of student teaching could be, as Goodlad[3] points out, one of the most useful parts of their teacher education preparation. Yet, they acknowledged that they would need help in extending and transforming the traditional experience of student teaching. This was just one more space for experimenting. With the establishment of the PDS internships, they saw the opportunity to experiment with the assistance of the Teachers College faculty.

There was a supervision course in the Curriculum and Teaching Program at TC that would become a space for theoretically based dialogue about supervision. The meetings at the school would be a space for working out the goals, processes, and methods associated with the PDS internships. This course became an academic requirement for the cooperating teachers before an intern was placed in their classrooms.

As the teachers engaged in discussions about improving teacher education, some teachers also felt they could, as clinical faculty, offer an element of practice to the College offerings. They knew that they had a handle on the setting, the students, and what worked for the student populations they taught. After all, they had helped the school go from the bottom of the education ranks to becoming a model school. They were successful in raising the student scores and changing the environment of the school. When Ruth entered the school, only 17 percent of the student body was on or above the school grade level. While the scores did not skyrocket, the school regularly had 32 percent of the school student population testing at or above their school grade level. Given this experience, the teachers felt they could assist the college in preparing the teachers who would be skilled in working with inner-city, minoritized language populations.

At the College, interest about the school had been growing. Numerous newspaper articles reported the drug cleanup in the neighborhood and the high levels of parent participation. The word was out that the school was dynamic and prevailing in transforming and improving education.[4]

The First Bilingual Internships

The following year, student teachers from many TC programs, such as TESOL, Curriculum and Teaching, Arts, and Science, roamed throughout the school and made it a home for at least one semester. Many of the teacher education programs were already involved with other PDS schools, but PS 165 represented a different setting with a new type of relationship.

Two bilingual interns were selected, and one completed the whole intern cycle before Ruth retired. The bilingual internship, at that time, was modeled on the preservice elementary program internship. The first semester, the student assumed the role of a regular student teacher but began preparing for taking greater responsibilities in January for two weeks, and in June for five weeks. The takeover of the classroom by the intern accomplished two objectives: The student teacher was able to gain broader experiences with the support of the cooperating teacher, staff developer, principal, intern supervisor, and instructor of the supervision course, and the cooperating teachers were released to do professional development. The internships were organized so that the teaching experience started earlier, was longer in duration, and was more structured than traditional student teaching.

Ruth asked me to guide the fourth-grade cooperating teachers' reflections on the process of supporting and supervising student teachers and interns during the first year of the PDS internship at PS 165. The PDS intern benefited from the knowledge of the instructor of student teaching, the supervising faculty, and the PDS supervisor. Simultaneously, the cooperating teachers took the supervision course, which I taught that year. I adapted the supervision course at the College for work with the fourth-grade team. It became their portfolio activity for the year.[5] The fourth-grade team did the readings, discussed the readings in relation to their supervision of the first bilingual intern at PS 165, and assessed their personal growth and development in light of their reflections about themselves as teachers and supervisors. It was a process of learning that used the authentic context of learning activity as an object of reflection.

I asked them to look at themselves and their concerns about having another adult in their classrooms who, in some ways, was also a student. I asked them to identify an area of the intern's weakness where they considered themselves strong. They were to do an in-class demonstration around the area or skill identified. The classroom teacher asked the student teacher to watch and participate in reflection on what had occurred. Then, the student teacher was to plan and implement a lesson that incorporated the area or skill, and to reflect on what occurred during his or her lesson with the teacher. The teacher's portfolio was the documentation not only of the student teacher's growth but also of his or her own process of growth and development as supervisors. At the end of the year, Ruth, upon reading the portfolio, called me up. She said, "I just finished reading the fourth-grade, dual-language teacher portfolio. I can see your influence coming through in the teachers' thinking. I wanted you to know it was great to see."

The collective experience of the first-year internship provided both the teachers and the program a space to reflect on the design and implementation of the College coursework and field experiences. The issues that arose were related to the greater complexity in the organization of language and instruction in the dual-language education program design. How could the bilingual placement be accomplished in the context of a team-teaching approach where languages were separated? And, because our commitment was to the native language placement, when would the English component teacher have a student teacher or intern? Would the student teacher/intern stay in one language or would they follow the children? How could we ensure a broad teaching experience for the prospective teachers if they were in one rather than in two schools for the duration of two semesters? What would be the trade-offs? All of these questions had to be answered jointly with the goal of preserving, protecting, and developing the native language of the children.

Intervisitations

Changes were also necessary in student teaching, as we had to differentiate it from the internships, while at the same time bring into it what knowledge we acquired that might improve it. Our teacher education students were asking many questions as well. Victoria "Tori" Hunt (1999), the PDS point person at PS 165, began to use this experience as a teacher inquiry for her portfolio. She was interested in how collaboration was promoted among student teachers and teachers. She chose to promote an intervention that came to be known as intervisitation that involved teachers (and other instructional personnel) visiting other teachers in the building. After the intervisitation, a reflective conversation would follow. Tori chose to study the intervisitation activities systematically.

She wanted to find out the extent of reflection and learning that came out of the activities.

Tori was one of the first three graduates of ours hired in the school. She was very familiar with reflective teaching and two years into the PDS formal partnership, she took on the responsibility of placing 25 student teachers from Teachers College and four other institutions. Her interest in the intervisitation arose because she believed this was "another space for reflection." She felt that visiting other classrooms had been very useful in her own growth and wanted to institutionalize it within the school.

The intervisitations were set up to promote better communication among teachers and to offer practicing teachers another way of engaging in critique and reflection. Tori believed that it was important to set up the intervisitations so that they would be nonthreatening and less intrusive. She had cooperating teachers accompany their student teachers in observing other teachers. She followed up by interviewing all those involved—the teacher observed, the cooperating teacher, and the student teacher/intern—jointly and individually.

When she analyzed the interviews, she found that interns acted more like teachers than student teachers. Student teachers focused on the teacher and the physical layout of the classroom. Interns, like teachers, focused mostly on the children. The two teachers-to-be groups also differed on how they talked about instructional techniques. While the student teachers talked about ways to copy practices in the future, the student interns and the teachers focused on how they could "adopt them" to their "own way of teaching."

Tori also found that for the practicing teachers this was an occasion to talk about what was happening in the school; they went beyond themselves and their classrooms. One teacher had paid attention to the consistency in the literacy approach throughout the school; another teacher realized that the native language time could be strengthened with new staffing patterns. Another began to see how the entire school was her responsibility.

Tori also observed that the shared experience created by the intervisitation became a basis for further and more intimate cooperation between the cooperating teacher and the student teacher or intern than in the past. She found out that one of the values of the intervisitation was that it became a way in which a teacher could receive genuine and professional acknowledgement. She envisioned PS 165 becoming a professional teaching institution.

Another aspect transformed by the intervisitation was the supervision of the student teachers and interns. After witnessing an intern, cooperating teacher, and supervisor come together for a supervision conversation following observation of a student teacher, Tori realized that within the intervisitation format, the induction of a new teacher became the responsibility of an expanded group.[6] It now included the PDS coordinator in the school, the school staff developer, the PDS liaison at the College, the instructor of the student teaching seminar who might not be the intern supervisor, and the intern supervisor. In addition, as the then-coordinator of the teacher education program, I was kept abreast on events and student teaching/intern issues, as the instructor of the student teaching seminar also attended program meetings. This expanded support ensured more frequent and sustained supervision for the teacher-to-be and timely feedback to the program faculty and involved administrators.

Tori's coordination of student teachers brought about the need for new spaces for conversations with the institutions of higher education about student teaching. The school called a meeting, requesting the presence of College faculty members to dialogue about student teaching. I was the only faculty member attending from TC, but faculty members from other institutions were present. I taped the meeting and consequently made it available to my colleagues. The teachers at PS 165 spoke to issues related to different programs in the College and to different colleges. A colleague from another institution and I felt that the issues raised by the teachers were thoughtful and had great merit. I felt it was another way in which we continued to tear down the walls between us. The profession of teaching was the business of a broader group, not just of me or the schools.

PDS Teaching Seminar

The student teaching/internship within the PDS schools in the district was different from the traditional forms of student teaching in other ways. First, within the partnership, there was an organized PDS seminar where teachers from the different PDS schools presented information to each other and to student teachers on their practices. They focused on different professional knowledge areas or subjects. All the student teachers in the PDS schools were invited to attend. The seminar experience provided teachers in preparation an expanded community with which to dialogue about the craft of teaching.

The second difference was that the bilingual student teachers were asked to participate in a teacher study group (either the dual-language or literacy study group) before going into the classroom. PDS interns had a bit more freedom. PDS interns decided what inquiry group they would attend in conjunction with the cooperating teacher with whom they would serve as bilingual interns. The work with the inquiry study groups provided student teachers/interns with an experience that went beyond the classroom to one that gave them a sense of the whole life of the school. Through the inquiry study groups the student teachers/interns also became part of the school community and their experience became the responsibility of all the participating teachers. This new structure also assisted in broadening the student teaching experience for those student teachers/interns who remained in the same school for two semesters.

PDS Inquiry Group

In the meantime, a PDS schoolwide inquiry group was born. In addition to the teacher inquiry projects, which were the center of its work, the group discussed partnership issues. One such item was the internship and how to be part of the selection of interns. For the most part, the university members of the partnership selected the interns. PS 165 teachers raised this as an issue. They felt they might have selected people other than the ones we had selected. A comparison between the school and university criteria signaled the institutional values emerging from each. While the College emphasized the academic potential of the student, at the school level the teacher group emphasized their experiences with children.

The disconnect we found between the teacher education program and school criteria led the teacher education faculty to look at potential candidates' experience with children and to create more explicit ways of judging a candidate's commitment to the field, including experience in working with children, working with minoritized language communities, and working in educational settings. This new consensus became an opportunity to streamline what we had always experienced as a very cumbersome admissions process. The weighting of prior experience with children also became an explicit criterion in the ranking of students for the PDS internships.

The following year, the teacher education program gave the PDS teachers of PS165 the criteria for ranking the applicants for our program (without names) and they then began to participate in the College's selection of interns for the school.

The Greater Council

The PDS had an executive council. The executive council meetings were attended by representatives of all the PDS schoolteachers and administrators, the faculty members involved in the school, and the PDS administrators from Teachers College and the school district. The executive council served to help coordinate some of the structures like the PDS intern seminar, the Greater Council meetings, Holmes Conference attendance and participation, and other policy-related issues.

The Greater Council was a forum for broader dialogue on PDS issues. We met three or four times a year. A theme was developed jointly. It usually focused on a substantive topic that we could not address as a group in the executive council. Teaching and administrative staff in the participating schools and college programs was invited to attend a full-day Greater Council work session.

Through the Greater Council, a charter for the PDS was developed in the 1998–1999 year. For PS 165 teachers, the creation of the charter coincided with Ruth's retirement; thus, it became a vehicle for the teachers to secure their stake in collaboration, reflection, and dialogue as means for teacher growth and development.

As part of the charter, each school developed annual goals. PS 165 teachers established their first annual goals as: (1) promoting teacher-generated action research; (2) collaboration between student teachers and cooperating teachers; (3) mentoring new teachers; (4) involving teachers in a public forum for teacher sharing, dialogue, and critique; and (5) involving the teachers in work within the world of research and college teaching.

The continuous engagement in reinventing of self that the PDS came to represent brought intellectual stimulation and energy to the school. It generated many public ways for teachers to share with other teachers and teacher educators across schools and nationally. The end-of-the-year PDS celebration involving all the members of the partnership was an instance of public performance initiated by the teachers of PS 165 only three months after Ruth's retirement. The PS 165 PDS group created an authentic local audience for teacher research. The school[7] hosted teachers in the TC/CSD#3 PDS Partnership to share the results of their teacher inquiries with other teachers in the school; teachers of other schools; and faculty, graduate students, and staff from Teachers College. This event became symbolic of their sense of community beyond school walls.

The Holmes Partnership Annual Conference

Finally, there was the Holmes Partnership Annual Conference. The teachers volunteered to present reports, sometimes jointly with faculty members, at the conference.[8] The time away from school with faculty and staff from the College occurred as a structured dialogue within the conference. The conference was organized so that this would occur. It provided a space for conversations across the school and program— conversations about the needs of the partnership.

It was at this conference that the teachers at PS 165 began to under-stand that the significance of their work extended beyond their school and their district. Not only did it give them a standard for judging their work, it also permitted them to see how far along they were in the process. Since bilingual teachers had primarily dominated the PDS at PS 165, I saw the conference as a great opportunity for integrating monolingual teachers. This made it unlike many other schools that have problems integrating the bilingual teaching personnel.

DISTURBING THE BILINGUAL TEACHER EDUCATION PROGRAM

The ongoing transformation of PS 165 was beginning to disturb the bilingual teacher education program. It became a two-way street. By the third year, a team of faculty and graduate students decided to study the fieldwork of the teacher preparation program.[9] They designed a case study of the field practices and found three salient themes: (1) the complexity of primary language instruction in schools versus the lack of primary language teaching at the College level, (2) the need for more hands-on examples of primary language instruction, and (3) the need to create a community of learners among teachers-to-be.

We discovered our graduate students' language discomfort or insecu-rity[10] with the native language of the children with whom they were to work. Some of our students were from the same language background as the children but they had not been schooled in the language. Thus, they felt insecure with respect to the academic language necessary to teach in it. Some of the students learned the language in which they were to teach as a second language. They felt uncomfortable speaking the languages of the children, other than English, in academic settings.

Our findings on language insecurities led to an immediate change in the student teaching seminar. The faculty members began to create native language instructional settings within the seminar. The initial attempt to offer the TC student teaching seminar and reading course in the majority language, Spanish, was short-lived, however. The experiment in native language instruction as the College level was possible when all of the seminar participants shared the language other than English, which was Spanish. The minute a student from one of the other five language groups in the program serviced came into the seminar, it was no longer possible.

There were other changes, however, like the native language component assessment that has been sustained in more systematic ways. Previously, the program had asked prospective students to provide evidence of language proficiency (through test scores, licensures, or other official ratings) and then conducted individual interviews or asked students to send in videotapes for us to review to verify the prospective students' proficiency. We already had a rating system (1 to 5) of language proficiency in the admissions process, but we realized the need to be more explicit about what constituted each rating. The follow-up on language proficiency within the admissions decision-making process also needed fine-tuning. Thus, rubrics were developed for evaluating oral proficiency in telephone and face-to-face interviews and for evaluating written responses to questions about teaching in general and in a bilingual setting in particular. By making the criteria more explicit, a language consultant could do the initial evaluation and questions could be brought up for discussion with the faculty members at the Admissions Committee level. This process was later institutionalized.

Another aspect of the native language component was related to advising. We annually asked students to work with their designated advisors on a plan for developing their language competency. The students were made responsible for improving their own language proficiencies so that they were at nativelike if not native levels of proficiency by the time they graduated. One of the ways to call attention to this was by developing language goals early in their teacher education programs. Course assignments were frequently in the native language of the children they would be teaching, and finally their student teaching would take place in that language.

The student teaching seminar also underwent social organizational changes that promoted greater exchange between students reflecting on each other's planning, demonstrating mini-lessons, discussing the consequences of theoretical conceptualizations in the structure of lessons, and implementing lessons with children (through videotape). The objectives were to deal with the need for developing professional knowledge or knowledge of practice and to foster a greater sense of community. The seminar attempted to model collaborative work and how ownership of one's own learning could be constructed in a community of learners. It attempted to develop an environment that permitted the students to explore issues of academic language and language variation as part of the lesson planning, demonstration, and implementation. There have been many different instructors for the seminar since then but some of these elements are still in place.

An additional issue that had concerned bilingual students and was partially examined by the case study was the issue of coordination and integration of the regular education and bilingual portions of their teacher preparation programs. Bilingual preservice students felt as though they were the "stepchildren" in the regular program. There was a lack of preparation for their arrival, they learned about requirements late, and they sometimes were required to complete work that they felt was unfair. During the case study, the regular preservice program faculty and the bilingual education faculty met to address these concerns in a spirit of collaboration. Admissions schedules were better aligned and communication lines were established. Bilingual students were grouped as a cohort within the regular preservice courses, and the preservice faculty began to address language issues more explicitly.

In general, the faculty members had to move from being at the center to being facilitators in their teaching, with more group work led by students. Prospective teachers became active learners in ways that could inform and influence their work with students in schools. Instead of just talking about the language issues, students were given hands-on opportunities to work through the language issues in relation to teaching. In addition, the structures between programs were better understood and measures to integrate them as a way to create community, while they are continuously revisited, were part of a continuous dialogue across programs.

OTHER WAYS OF BREAKING ISOLATION AND CREATING COMMUNITY

A consequence of the school/university partnership was that the schools and the university broke with their insularity. The teachers of the different schools began to engage in a variety of forums that promoted what Lieberman[11] calls teachers in public performance. This gave the teachers new ways of channeling their creative energies.

One such way was by fostering relationships between teachers across schools in the same district. This enriched PS 165 and the other schools in immeasurable ways. For example, one of the teachers from PS 87 came to visit PS 165 with her whole class. PS 87 is well-known as a white and upper-middle-class school with great resources that had been the original PDS school in the partnership. When the teachers and students from PS 84 visited PS 165, they were very impressed by the beauty of the school, by the quality of the student work displayed, and by the dignity of its students. PS 165 students, in turn, went to visit PS 87; they felt the same way about that school. The result was a curricular change of significance; the two classes became pen pals throughout the school year, and the exchange visits created very concrete and authentic audiences for student writings.

The PDS created a variety of opportunities for PS 165 staff to offer their expertise in second language issues to teachers of other schools. They participated in a TC-organized exchange among teachers in the district, exchanging their expert knowledge for knowledge in other areas, such as math and social studies. The cross-school collaboration, whether it involved students or teachers, created opportunities for reflection and curricular change that pushed the continued growth of the teachers at PS 165.

In addition to the Holmes Partnership Annual Conferences, other national conferences, such as the annual meeting of the American Educational Research Association (AERA), become important forums for teachers to display their work and their thinking. The conferences were viewed as opportunities for teachers to disseminate information on what they do as part of their professional development and in relation to the education of minoritized language students. The April 2000 AERA presentation by two of the teachers embodied what Bullough Jr. and his colleagues[12] call boundary spanning. Both teachers were former students of the Program in Bilingual/Bicultural Education and they had become school leaders at PS 165. They continued to take graduate courses and worked as clinical faculty at the College. I had been scheduled to attend and present at AERA but was unable to do so. I felt these two teachers were at a stage of development where they could present on my behalf. One of the teachers, Amanda Hartman, was a teacher leader in the TC Writing Project, taught the native language literacy course for the bilingual teacher education program, was the leader of the literacy study group in the school, and was the school liaison for research on best practices with the Documentation and Dissemination Initiative of the New York

City Board of Education in which Brown University, Teachers College, and Hunter College were participants. She spoke about these new relationships of collaboration and their relationship to teacher growth. The second teacher was the PDS liaison, Victoria Hunt, whom I have mentioned earlier. She focused on her work organizing the school as a learning space for new teachers from different institutions of higher learning. She presented on her documentation of intervisitations.

When these two teachers came back from AERA, they did so with gained appreciation for the significance of what was happening at PS 165. They had understood their roles as genuine leaders in the field. They had heard others present and had been able to craft meaningful comparisons between their own experiences and what they heard others say while at the conference. "We are leaders!" they came back reporting. Their experiences disseminating what they knew validated their knowledge and their ability to forge new ways of thinking.

REFLECTION ON FREEDOM: THE INDIVIDUAL AND THE COLLECTIVE

The images of freedom created in the professional development as freedom section focused on the relationships between the individual and the collective; they also raise the issues of constraints, obstacles, and responsibilities. I have perhaps focused more on the positive examples than on the obstacles and constraints, but the latter were there also. I have chosen not to dwell on them as I wanted to focus on the collaborative structures that permitted teachers to face obstacles and constraints in less individualistic and lonely ways.

Ruth was willing to set up structures of support that gave the teachers the freedom to be professionals and to exercise their autonomy in creative ways. While the teachers had freedom to exercise their autonomy as teachers, they were also responsible for delivery—as evidenced in their reporting on their students' and their own progress. The teacher, while being acknowledged for his or her strengths, had the responsibility of engaging in professional activities that consciously and deliberately dealt with his or her own individual weaknesses. How to do away with constraints, perceived or real, that inhibit teachers from doing their best for the children they served was also put on the table. This environment set up a relationship of generosity and exigency on both sides. Teachers began to more willingly take on activities beyond teaching that helped them move into a posture of agency where they could reflect on their own classroom practices with the whole group and the individual children and to see how their understanding of theories, their observations, and their conceptualizations of learning for the population that was learning in two languages were part problem and/or solution to the improvement of learning. In other words, they were moving to assume responsibility for their teaching in the context of both intellectual and social freedom.

Furthermore, the relationship of generosity and freedom was accompanied by inclusiveness and expansion of the realms of participation possible within the school. Thus, freedom and participation came to the fore. As teachers and parents became more involved in what happened at the school, they also began to assume a shared responsibility in the process and outcome of the life at PS 165. In assuming this relationship the usual personality and ego conflicts that sometimes stunt school initiatives were diminished. As people are human, there were times when their egos were on the table, but by reminding each other of the larger purpose and reminding each other that they were experimenting, many personally paralyzing situations were averted or ameliorated. Thus, a larger number of adults were rallied to work jointly for the improvement of the education of the children the school served.

We explored the structures and groups in which the teachers developed professionally. They were diverse and, for the most part, voluntary in nature. Teachers chose to participate, to initiate, and to lead in the different group structures. It is my assertion that these forms of professional development called for school norms that enhanced the individual teacher's freedom to develop his or her capabilities. In this sense, it mirrored Sen's analysis of development where "attention is paid particularly to the expansion of the 'capabilities' of persons to lead the kind of lives they value—have reason to value."[13] Self-interest may have motivated the teachers' self-improvement as teachers. I do not doubt this at all. Yet, much of the discourse of the teachers is of a higher order. In the dual-language study group experience, for example, there is some evidence that the norms and practices of the group were inspiring to individuals within the group. As a group, they agreed to take on the responsibility of an advocacy stance for minoritized language children rather than on insisting on their individual ways. They called on each other to give up familiar and individually preferred ways of speaking for an academic standard in solidarity with each other as teachers with a social commitment to create classroom environments that would help bring "capabilities" and, thus, freedom to others—the students. The freedoms to participate, to voice, to speak, and to choose were achieved through conscious collective engagement.

In the collaborative structures, teachers and others came together "as equals" in relation to the school goals—to reflect upon, name, and transform what was; to explore, discover, and create alternatives about their wonderings and their concerns; and to imagine different ways of understanding. The relationship between freedom and responsibility came up when teachers brought in their frustrations about a student, the difficulties of implementing a new curriculum mandate, the need to role play a conversation with a parent, and the joy of seeing a child opening up to them. The conversations were not the usual self-help approach that we encounter, as the teachers did not hold the individual as solely responsible for all that happened to her or to him. Yet, they embraced the need for individual agency, where the individual chose to participate or not in improving his or her own capabilities to address the professional day-to-day pathologies that plague a teacher's life. They also embraced the reality that improving their own lives affected and engaged others in the act of making a reality of the improvement that they desired.

Agency, as the ability to stand for oneself, is constrained by social, political, and economic factors within the domains of work in which an individual is engaged. The teachers, for example, needed a space in which they could explore their individual freedom while retaining a sense of being part of a concerted effort that shared principles or shared conceptions of what is good and right for bilingual children. It was not just an individual teacher engaged in figuring out what he or she needed to do. Instead, they were individual teachers within a collective structure and, in concert with the leadership of the school and the school's support networks, they made a difference in other people's lives.

In the *Dialectics of Freedom*, Maxine Greene explores freedom as the thinking we do when we detach and reflect upon that which we do in the world and as the voicing we do when we want to speak in the "sphere of freedom."[14] It is not just the thinking; it is also the voicing that occurs in reflective circles such as the study groups. When an individual shares his or her thoughts with others, thinking individually becomes collective. What is done jointly simultaneously becomes the property of the group and the individual. Freedom, in this context, is not just the capability of being free; it is also acting on freedom, individually and collectively, to achieve that which was desired. When acting in freedom, an opening for new action exists. Thus, we can say that at PS 165, development of teachers did show up as freedom.[15]

According to Sen, "individual freedom is quintessentially a social product, and there is a two-way relation between (1) social arrangements to expand individual freedoms and (2) the use of individual freedoms not only to improve the (sic) respective lives but also to make the social arrangements more appropriate and effective."[16]

ACTIVITIES

1. Reflect on your service learning, field work, or student teaching experiences. Did you have a group of colleagues that helped you reflect on your experience with teaching? Imagine you could improve your ability to reflect with a group of people. With whom would it occur? Write a letter to the coordinator/chair of your teachers education program and communicate your proposal for creating a structure that would promote greater reflection in the program.

2. You have been asked by your neighborhood district to put together a list of five topics for a series of workshops about working with bilingual children that veteran teachers could offer to novice teachers. Talk to at least ten classmates about what they would like to get directly from those who work with the bilingual children you are likely to teach. Report to the class on your findings.

ENDNOTES

1. The TC/CSD #3 Professional Development School Partnership was an outgrowth of the Holmes Group, a national consortium of research institutions dedicated to improving schools through shifting perspectives on teacher preparation, professionalizing teaching, engaging in teacher inquiry, and restructuring colleges of education.

2. Darling-Hammond, Linda. "Developing Professional Development Schools: Early Lessons, Challenges, and Promises," in L. Darling-Hammond (ed.), *Professional Development Schools: Schools for Developing a Profession* (New York: Teachers College Press, 1994, pp. 1–27).

3. Goodlad, James I. *Teachers for Our Nation's Schools.* (San Francisco: Jossey Bass, 1990).

4. Richardon, Lynda. "Mission Possible: Reviving a Dying Public School" *New York Times,* June 20, 1995, Section B1.

5. In addition, the teachers received three credits from Teachers College (TC), Columbia University. TC had a special arrangement with the PDS schools. Each student teacher they supervised meant that their school was granted a voucher of three credits. The teachers I worked with were not paid but received three credits

from the accumulated pool of credits of the school. For me, the author of the text, this work with the teachers counted toward one of the four courses I had to teach annually.

6.   Since part of Tori's job was to be the school liaison for the PDS and other institutions of higher education, there was no extra pay for this additional work. In some other schools, there were individuals on grants who played this role.

7.   The activity was organized by the PS 165 teachers as an after-school activity with coffee and snacks within the school building.

8.   Both the CSD#3 and TC funded the PDS participants attending the conference. Sometimes grant travel money was used. We were all encouraged to be frugal so that as many of the participants could attend as possible.

9.   Rubio, Olga, Teresa Lopez-Marquez, and Lucia Rodriguez. *A Collaborative Case Study of Preservice Bilingual Teachers: Implications for Curricular and Administrative Change.* Unpublished manuscript, n.d. This study was partially funded by grants.

10.   Labov, William. *Sociolinguistic Patterns.* (Philadelphia: University of Pennsylvania Press, 1972); Zentella, Ana Celia. *Growing up Bilingual in El Barrio.* (Cambridge, UK: Cambridge University Press, 1998).

11.   Lieberman, Ann, and Linda Friedrich. "Teachers, Writers, Leaders." *Educational Leadership* 6, 1 (2007): 42–47.

12.   Bullough, Robert V., Jr., Donald P. Kauchak, Nedra A. Crow, Sharon Hobbs, and David Stokes. "Long-term PDS Development in Research Universities and the Clinicalization of Teacher Education." *Journal of Teacher Education,* 48 (1997): 85–95

13.   Sen, Amartya. *Development as Freedom.* (New York: Random House, 1999), p. 18.

14.   Arendt, Hanna. *The Human Condition.* (Chicago: University of Chicago Press, 1958, p. 30) cited in Greene, *Dialectics of Freedom,* p. 3.

15.   Sen, *Development as Freedom.*

16.   Id. at 31.

7

TEACHING AS SOCIAL PRACTICE

⊷

The teachers' concerns came through in how they expressed their curiosity about curriculum and instruction. Within the dual-language education program, the understanding that there were cultural and linguistic differences among students made these wonderings more specific to children who came into the school speaking languages other than English. These children faced the need to learn or improve their proficiencies in both the language of the home, Spanish, and a second language, that is, in the language of the school, English. In the previous chapters, we looked at freedom as personally realized within social relationships and structures. In this chapter, we focus on how the teachers find the seeds of freedom as they work to see children blossom or struggle to blossom as human and academic beings. The focus is on their work as curriculum and learning theorists—as the developers of curriculum, the instructors, and the reflective practitioners. Where in the curriculum did they find or struggle to make the spaces for bilingualism and multiculturalism? How did their curriculum and instruction planning and implementation embody the intuitive, intellectual, and experiential understandings that helped them provide children with environments where they could freely access the two linguistic systems for learning? How did they take what the children brought—their language, culture, and the social beliefs that undergird ingenuous curiosity and make learning, meaning freedom in thinking, happen? How did they set up those cultural and linguistic environments so students would engage in epistemological curiosity? Where did they find the seeds of and for freedom, and what were some of the constraints that concerned the teachers?

I selected five cases that represent aspects of freedom within the areas of curriculum development, instruction, and teacher reflection. There were many wonderful incidents, situations, and projects from which I could have chosen. There were many occasions in which the struggle was superior to the finding of ways to sow seeds of freedom. However, the five vignettes were selected because they illustrate how teachers can choose to stand in freedom as they engage in the education of culturally and linguistically diverse students. These examples also represent a range of teaching situations—from Spanish to English, from early childhood to all levels—that are bound by their focus on the language and cultural aspects the teachers faced in their everyday lives in classrooms, whether monolingual or bilingual. There were other topics I might have chosen, but my focus on the bilingual children colors this presentation. Within the principal's chapter she will talk about other areas on which the teachers as a whole were focusing. Less important, although critical for this book, is that I observed and/or worked directly with the teachers involved.

CASE #1: ON CULTURE AND CURRICULUM

Isabel, a monolingual kindergarten Latina teacher, was active in the Professional Development School relationship with the College. She had engaged in a variety of inquiry projects with which I assisted, as I usually worked with the methodological aspects of the projects. Her ability to plan, develop, and follow through on sophisticated issues around curriculum had impressed me. Thus, when the opportunity to develop a presentation on multiple languages, multiple cultures, and equity at a national level came up,[1] I asked her to work with me. The entire national project was much broader, as it extended from early childhood to institutions of higher education. It also covered bilingual and monolingual situations. Within my segment of the project, Isabel was tasked to develop the example of multiculturalism within the early childhood monolingual Pre-K curriculum.

In this example, Isabel attempted to develop cultural expression and engagement among her diverse group of students. She chose to illustrate how she planned around the theme of foods. She planned a culturally responsive curriculum resulting in the creation of new spaces for cultural infusion in all the subject areas, taking into account the standards in each of the subject areas for this grade level (See Figure 7.1). In doing so, she also created spaces for alternative interpretations.

Isabel designed the illustrated web and shared with me a pattern of thinking about lessons that helped her bring forth and infuse cultural expression and engagement into all her lessons. She starts with a few assessment tools that she has developed over the years. These can be in the form of questionnaires to parents, based on thematic readings, compositions, and/or reflective discussions. She was guided by two concepts: connectivity and challenging stereotypes.

The first concept was designed to consciously occur. She made connections with the parents and the neighborhood cultural institutions in order to construct the lessons. She then engaged the rest of the school and others in the extended community by organizing ways in which the children shared what they had done.

Figure 7.1: Isabel's Food Study Curricular Map

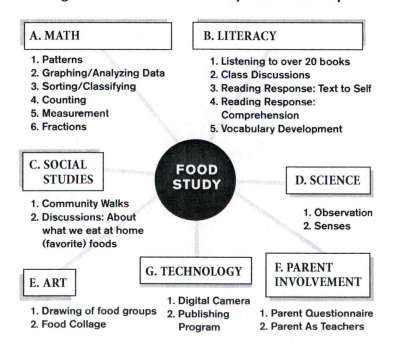

A. MATH
1. Patterns
2. Graphing/Analyzing Data
3. Sorting/Classifying
4. Counting
5. Measurement
6. Fractions

B. LITERACY
1. Listening to over 20 books
2. Class Discussions
3. Reading Response: Text to Self
4. Reading Response: Comprehension
5. Vocabulary Development

FOOD STUDY

C. SOCIAL STUDIES
1. Community Walks
2. Discussions: About what we eat at home (favorite) foods

D. SCIENCE
1. Observation
2. Senses

E. ART
1. Drawing of food groups
2. Food Collage

G. TECHNOLOGY
1. Digital Camera
2. Publishing Program

F. PARENT INVOLVEMENT
1. Parent Questionnaire
2. Parent As Teachers

Two parental surveys were sent home. The first was a survey that requested that the parents send to school recipes from their heritage background or the home country. The second was a request for volunteers to come into the classroom to cook with the children. She met with the parent volunteers to discuss the ingredients, the shops where they bought the ingredients, and how the cooking lesson would occur in the classroom. They were also asked to help develop a multicultural cookbook with the recipes they would cook with the children and the ones that other parents sent. Thus, the parents were brought into the classroom as cultural experts (transmitting the culture of the home) and the knowledge they brought with them as an intellectual resource for the classroom.

Before the lesson, the children would go on community walks to buy the ingredients with the parent volunteers, the teaching assistant, and the teacher. In connecting with the shops and restaurants, some of the external institutions to the school within the community were also set up as sources of cultural knowledge, as information providers, and as part of the power structure in their communities.

The second principle, challenging stereotypes, sometimes came in unanticipated places. To prepare the children for the different aspects of the food study unit, the teacher selected over 20 books to read to the young children. She had many discussions with the children about foods. The children sorted plastic food from the playhouse area into four categories (fruits and vegetables, meats, breads, milk and dairy). The children then selected one of the foods to draw for their "four basic food groups" mural. The teacher helped them create webs of the different types of foods they liked. They made drawings and collages of food types and favorite foods. For example, after reading Seuss's *Green Eggs and Ham*,[2] the children did polling and graphing. The children predicted whether they would like the taste of green eggs and ham. The teacher asked them to draw a happy face on a circle if they thought they would like it or a sad face if they thought they would not like it. Five children drew sad faces because they could not eat ham—they were Muslims. While Isabel may have not anticipated where she would challenge stereotypes, she was keenly alert to recognize and address them. Before moving on, she stopped to discuss the issue of culture, religion, and foods that were present in the classroom. She told them that during work time they would make green eggs without ham in order to accommodate everyone. By example, she demonstrated tolerance and adaptation. Everyone tasted the green eggs and drew another face indicating their likes or dislikes of the eggs. The class interpreted the graph by counting how many people thought they would like the green eggs and how many actually liked them. The amount of people who changed their opinions was also compared.

After reading *Feast for 10,* the teacher asked the children to engage in a text-to-self discussion by asking them how they ate dinner in their own homes. Following the discussion, she asked them to draw detailed pictures of dinner at home. This became a space for the children to speak about the typical foods and the family dynamics around foods as alternatives to what was presented in the written text.

The children drew pictures to answer the question "what happened in the story?" after listening to *Too Many Tamales* several times to develop reader responses and check for comprehension. Isabel wrote what she did:

Day 1: We read the story as a "just listen" read. (no discussion)
   Day 2: We took a picture walk and used the illustrations to retell the story. (discussion, review)
   Day 3: We reread the story, stopping for comments. After we finished, the children drew a picture to answer a question. The teacher/teacher assistant took dictation from the children.

Dictation was a regular staple in this classroom as the children do not generally have the motor or literacy skills developed to do their own writing at this age. Yet, it was important to affirm and capture their ideas in text form so as to expose the children to a fundamental aspect of authorship, like having something to say. For book reviews, for example, the teacher read the book individually to the child, and captured, through dictation, the child's opinion about the book; the child would complete the review by drawing a picture of his or her favorite part.

With respect to vocabulary development, during the entire food study unit, many new vocabulary words were introduced within the context of the activities. Some of the cooking utensils, for example, were labeled as "grater," "wok," "corer," "can opener," and so forth. When the cooking started, the teacher introduced the names of the utensils as they came up. The names of the foods also served to introduce new vocabulary such as "kiwi," "seaweed," "plantains," "tortilla," and "mango."

Isabel had the children work on patterns of fruits (apple, banana, pear, and orange) that they had to color and cut out as part of their math lessons. Two children worked with one adult. One of the adults reviewed the class chart, "What Did We Learn About Patterns" from which children engaged in a follow-up pattern activity using the fruits of their choice. While cooking, the children used measuring spoons and cups to achieve the objective of adding the correct amount of ingredients to the various recipes cooked in class. They compared a cup, half a cup, a tablespoon, and a teaspoon. They repeated this experience throughout the food study unit. Even the concept of fractions was introduced during the cooking activities. When they made *mangú,* a regular staple in a Dominican home, they worked with the whole and half concept. The plantains were peeled whole, and then cut in half for boiling.

Isabel shared her curriculum development and instruction of the unit with me. We jointly analyzed the culturally responsive teaching aspects found in her lesson. We found them in topic choice, in the parent questionnaire, in book choices, in the lesson—dishes, recipes, ingredients, utensils—and in the activities she assigned, such as drawings about dinner at home.

We also examined the curriculum for what was specifically cultural in it. We agreed that the food theme was a natural for examining culture, but we wanted to identify specifically where these aspects were visible. We found that she was able to get at cultural knowledge by focusing the home survey on the favorite foods from the heritage background or home country. It was not just a question about favorite foods; the survey asked about foods from a heritage background or from the home country. The expectation was that there would be distinctly different foods because the children were diverse. It was also information that all the children's parents and, thus, the children themselves, were able to contribute. The cultural artifacts they used were in utensils, such as the wok, and in the ingredients, such as the plantain. Some of these artifacts were new to some of the children, setting up the possibility of children learning from each other. Engaging the parents and the community institutions as cultural experts was also significant as they communicated inclusive values and worth. Isabel was cognizant that dialogue, poll taking, charts of preferences, and acts of tolerance were all part of instilling in the children democratic values. Exposure to other cultural values was structured through the readings and assigned tasks as well as by giving the issues that came up in the classroom a space for conversation. Finally, we identified the process of cultural affirmation and transformation in which the class participated as they took pictures during their walks, visits, and classroom work, and later constructed with the teacher and her assistants a collage depicting their experiences as they engaged in creating the multicultural cookbook for their homes and for others in the school.

I chose the example of Isabel's prekindergarten curriculum because it captured the spaces of freedom the teacher has available to create educational environments that can afford the freedoms necessary for student learning to take place. I agree with Banks[3] when he points out that "multicultural education is an education for freedom in three important senses: (1) it enables students to freely affirm their ethnic, racial, and cultural identities; (2) it provides students with the freedom to function beyond their ethnic and cultural boundaries; and (3) it helps students to develop the commitment and skills needed to participate in personal, social, and civic action that will make our nation and world more democratic and free." Isabel created an environment that had the spaces for individual children to affirm who they were within the worlds of foods. They learned about each other. And they participated in activities that not only engaged them in ways they would later experience as part of a democratic system, but also in the social experiences of promoting and respecting diversity.

Going back to Sen's proposition that the evaluations of freedoms must attend not just to the process but the outcomes, what Isabel was able to accomplish through her unbounded thinking about curriculum was to establish a place, physical and intellectual, that was safe and free for the children to engage with the topic, thus, learning about democratic ways and transforming their ingenuous curiosity into an epistemological one as well.

CASE #2: NEGOTIATING ACADEMIC LANGUAGE THROUGH CULTURE

Berta was then a dual-language, second-grade teacher; she was the part of the team that taught the Spanish component. I went to observe her on a day when she was doing a read aloud on *Sadako and the Thousand Paper Cranes*.[4] She sat on her teacher chair reading, and the children sat on the rug in front of her, listening to what Berta read to them. What struck me about Berta was her ability to connect aspects of the traditional cultures of the children with the story. I have observed her extensively in read aloud situations subsequently and have documented the enriching ways in which she engages children.[5] At times I could see how meaning and symbolism were elegantly unlocked and released by the words she spoke, but one has to look very carefully to see how she masterfully engaged children in the discovery of understanding meaning. In the story she was reading aloud, belief systems are very important and "superstition" is the "schooled word" she wanted them to understand. Berta stopped her reading various times to talk about the beliefs the characters held. The following interaction occurred after a discussion about the main character, when one of the students identified Sadako as being astute.

Teacher: *Es astuta porque le hizo un truco (o trampa) a su hermano. Es inteligente porque aprendió a hacer las grullas enseguida. Es una persona que cree en muchas cosas que le van a ayudar. ¿Cuántos conocen la palabra* supersticiosa? *Yo encuentro que Sakaro es supersticiosa. Les voy a dar una pista. Ella cree en las arañas, ella cree en el cielo sin nubes, ella cree que si hace 1,000 grullas, se va a curar.* [She is astute because she tricked her brother. She is intelligent because she learned quickly how to make paper cranes. She is a person who believes that many things will help her. How many of you know what "superstition" means? I find Sadako is superstitious. I will give you a hint. She believes in spiders, she believes in the sky without clouds, she believes that if she makes 1,000 paper cranes, she will be cured.]

The students responded by talking to each other. They made connections with their beliefs. The teacher continued the explanation.

Teacher: *Yo soy supersticiosa. O, si. Si yo paso por el funeral, yo digo so-lavaya, solavaya, solavaya.* [I am superstitious. Oh, yes. If I pass a funeral house, I say alone you go, alone you go, and alone you go.]

Student 1 (girl): *O, si.* [Oh, yes.]

Teacher: *Cuando yo veo un gato negro, me hago la cruz. Yo no quiero la mala suerte.* [When I see a black cat, I make the sign of the cross. I do not want bad luck to come upon me.]

The children broke out in animated chatter about the cultural connections of the teacher; they were making meaning of the word "superstitious" and the importance it had in their own lives.

The connection Berta made between the culturally specific forms of superstition found in the story, which pointed to the main character's personality and the students' lives, and the funeral home or the black cat examples seemed to detach the children's thinking from being focused on the specific words to focus on the word's meaning. She moved the children away from the lexical and cultural bindings of the story, permitting them to engage in getting at central aspects of the story and the character. In this way, the children moved to make the story and the academic language (as in "superstitious") of the story familiar and, thus, their own. She tapped on linguistic and cultural systems that are available to the bilingual child to mediate comprehension and vocabulary development.

As Bialystok points out, bilingual children operate with a certain lexical sensitivity through which they communicate their understanding that the relationship between concepts and words is "a convention, not a necessity; an agreement, not the truth" rather than the inherent meaning that a word has for the monolingual counterpart. As Bialystok states: "We are free to break the agreement if we so choose."[6] Berta was able, momentarily at least, to release the children from the agreement so that they could explore in their lived experiences similar concepts that would connect with that of the story.

CASE #3: TEACHING ACADEMIC LANGUAGE IN CONTEXT

Rebecca is a dual-language teacher in charge of the Spanish component in first grade. She was a student in the Programs in Bilingual/Bicultural Education at TC and an active teacher in the Professional Development School relationship with the College. She had been teaching a few years before this particular observation. I observed her early one morning during a literacy lesson. It was a well-planned lesson. Everything was organized and readily available for all the transitions she anticipated. What most impressed me about this lesson was how she reversed roles so that the children took on the role of experts in the language. This was particularly impressive because the subject was on conventions in writing and self-corrections. Obviously, it was a lesson in which already learned items were integrated for reinforcement.

> Teacher: OK. *Buenos días, niños y niñas.* [Good morning boys and girls.]
> As she speaks, she writes the phrase on the chart paper. In her writing, she does not include the tildes on the two second *n*s of the words *"niños"* [boys] and *"niñas"* [girls].
> Student 1 (boy): *Le falta el gorrito.* [The hat is missing.]
> Teacher: *¿Qué le falta?* [What is missing?]
> She looks around before she calls on a student; she praises a student who is following the rules.
> Teacher: *Me gusta como esta X.* [I like how X is behaving.]
> When she calls on a student, the student, pointing to the "n" says

Student 2 (boy): *Ahi tiene que tener un gorrito.* [You need a hat there.]

The teacher corrects the verb "*tener*"; it is a subtle correction.

Teacher: *Ahi tiene que poner un gorrito.* [You need to put a hat on.]

She puts the tilde on the first "n."

Student 3 (girl): *No!*

The teacher looks at the writing.

Teacher: *En la segunda "n"? Muchas veces se nos olvidan, se nos olvidan los sombreritos.* [On the second "n"? Frequently, we forget to put the little hats.]

Student 4 (boy): *Iba a decir nino y nina.* [You were going to say "nino" and "nina."]

Teacher: *No iba a sonar bien.* [It was not going to sound right.]

In this lesson, Rebecca's indirect way of teaching orthography was to relinquish her role as sole expert in the classroom and loosen up the traditional hierarchy between teacher and student. She situated herself so that the children would correct her. She was not only reviewing a writing convention, she was permitting the children to demonstrate their school knowledge. The lesson became somewhat humorous and enjoyable for the children. Furthermore, one of the students was able to articulate the orthographic rule, that is, why it was necessary to put the "hat" on by making reference to the relationship between sound and meaning. In essence, what the child said was that without the tilde, the words would not only sound wrong, the words would also be devoid of meaning.

Aside from an environment encouraging nontypical roles, it was a lesson that captured a first-grader's awareness of a sound/symbol relationship. It has been documented that the awareness of sound/symbol relationships among bilingual children develops at a faster pace than among their monolingual counterparts, as they have to master a broader range of phonemes corresponding to two languages. The struggle Spanish/English bilingual children have with the range of sounds is in the doubling up of symbols for different sounds that shows up when the child moves into literacy and the confusion that occurs when two symbols sound the same or one symbol has more than one sound. It is a constraint and an issue to which the teacher must pay attention. Clarity and distinctions between the languages are important here. For the teacher, what may be most important to understand is that what often is seen as a weakness comes from a strength—the child's ability to draw on two distinct phonemic systems. If we look at the range of phonemes the children bring with their bi/multilingualism as a strength, then we can turn the difficulty into one of pushing the bilingual child to develop in some areas that are not necessarily available with monolingual learners.

CASE #4: LANGUAGE CHOICE

Committing the teacher to the separation of the language of instruction in the dual-language education program did not mean the children were required to speak all the time in the day's language of instruction. There was some leeway for the students. The teachers encouraged the students to speak to the teacher and to their classmates in the more public settings in the language of instruction. Some of the students could not do so as they did not possess this proficiency. They might be newcomers to the country on the English day and/or dominant in English on the Spanish day. The teachers were to be sensitive to the latter while encouraging them little by little to say what they knew in the second language. The teacher was encouraged to repeat what the student had said in the language of the day to remind and push them, particularly in the weaker language. In addition, within small groups or in pairs of children, the language of conversations between them was to be their choice. The following is an example of what might occur among the students.

After reading *Kike,*[7] the fourth-grade, dual-language teacher asked the students to complete one of three tasks: a crossword puzzle, an advertisement, or a caricature. While they were each to develop their own instrument, they could talk, consult, and help each other. In the following group, four Dominican bilingual children were working together. Two girls were negotiating the task:

Lucia: (to Susana) *¿qué vas hacer?* [What are you going to do?]
Susana: *Un anuncio.* [An advertisement.]
Lucia: *Hagamos un crucigrama.* [Let's do a crossword puzzle.] We can work together.
Susana: *No puedo. Yo tengo mi anuncio en mi cabeza.* [I can't. I already have my advertisement in my head.]
Lucia: *Hagamo' el crucigrama.* [Let's do the crossword puzzle.] Please.
Susana: I said no.
Lucia: *Es que yo no sé hace' un crucigrama y tú sí.* [The thing is that I don't know how to do a crossword puzzle and you do.]
Susana: *Pero yo voy hace' un anuncio. To' lo' del grupo vamo' hacer' anuncio, meno' tú. Asi que es mejo' que te cambie' de group. SX 'tá haciendo*

un crucigrama. Vete a ese group. [But I am going to do an advertisement. All the group is going to do an advertisement, except you. SX is doing crossword puzzles. Go to that group.]

Lucia: *No. Mejor voy hacer un anuncio* [No. I think it is better to do an advertisement.]

In the above interaction, the two girls show their comfort in either of the languages. Lucia[8] uses both Spanish and English throughout to try to convince Susana to do a crossword puzzle. It is as if Susana, who apparently has more power in the group than Lucia, does not know English as well as Lucia. Lucia repeats what she said in Spanish and English in turn 1. In turn 3, English is used to present the rationale that might appeal to Susana. Lucia begs Susana to change her mind in turn 5. Finally, in turn 7, Lucia appeals to Susana's intellectual power. She acknowledges that she does not know how to do the crossword puzzle and would like some help from Susana. Up to the sixth turn, Susana responds in Spanish. She then switches to English. Susana's negation of Lucia's request in English seemed to indicate that if Lucia did not understand it in Spanish, she would say it in English so that there would be no mistake. She demonstrated she was bilingual, and her use of Spanish may be due to her dominance in the language or her choice to speak the language of the day.

Two items were important in the kind of environment created for bilingual learners in this dual-language education classroom. One was the students' abilities in the uses of both languages, and the other was around language choice.

Grosean[9] proposes that bilinguals engage in a range of language functions, each of which varies on a dimension from monolingual mode. The variation is usually the ability to incorporate both languages in their communications. In this example, Lucia switches languages for a variety of functions—she uses language in an instrumental way ("I want.") to indicate what she would like to do; she tries to make sure she is understood, when she tries to persuade Susana using interactional language ("me and you"). Susana changes code only to communicate and emphasize an assertion. Their language mixing and switching is normal and comprehensible. This free movement in the languages responds to social and linguistic circumstances within the interaction.

All children, as they develop linguistically, experience a level of language choice. For the bilingual, however, language choice has an added dimension of bilinguality. Grosean[10] calls it the bilingual view. The underlying linguistic competence in the two languages permits this movement. It also indicates that linguistic representation for bilinguals is importantly different from that of monolinguals. In other words, linguistic ability leads to language choice.

The dual-language education program, while keeping the languages separate academically, provides the kind of freedom Alzaldua[11] cries out for when she writes:

> Ethnic identity is twin skin to linguistic identity—I am my language. Until I can take pride in my language, I cannot take pride in myself.... I cannot accept the legitimacy of myself.... [A]s long as I have to accommodate the English speakers rather than having them accommodate me, my tongue will be illegitimate.

These emotions and connections can be made in the process of learning and using the two languages to perform academically. In the next case, we will see how the bilingual children at PS 165 find the freedom to stretch their linguistic expression in a monolingual classroom.

CASE #5: LEARNING ABOUT SCAFFOLDING

Peter is the monolingual computer specialist in the school. He has a computer lab where teachers take the children, but he also works directly with teachers. Peter was also an active member of the Professional Development School; he participated in many of the technology projects. In the focus situation, Peter was working with two second-grade dual-language education teachers. I referred to this project earlier. It was the team that was doing an inquiry project on language transfer. He was helping them document their inquiry project by capturing and videotaping the teachers' request.

That year, Peter decided that his teaching portfolio would focus on what he learned from working with these two teachers about working with bilingual children. He set up his pedagogical inquiry questions as the following: "As a computer teacher, how might Hyperstudio be introduced and taught in an effective manner to students who vary significantly in the abilities and states of language transfer? What procedures might be used?"

Peter seized the opportunity to do inquiry with two of his dual-language colleagues. He set up the camcorder and hidden microphones for the book talks in the dual-language second grade. He also sat in the meetings to review the videotaping with the teachers. It was an occasion for him to learn about dual language and the transfer of languages. About the then newly acquired knowledge, he wrote:

> Considering I am a new teacher in New York City Public Schools, the knowledge I gained in this project about dual language and language transfer is a significant factor toward enhancing my ability to achieve success in my new environment.

He also learned to observe the children's responses to his instructions. About the language transfer of the three children who were the focus of the inquiry, he wrote the following:

> I documented that students' knowledge of the English language directly affected their ability to understand my explanation of the keywords since I always explained in English. For example, Luis learned at a slower rate, which was evidenced to me when he explained the keywords to his classmates. Importantly, I was able to ask Andrew or Marji to explain certain words and phrases in Spanish to him. In the end, his English explanation of the same became clearer. I concluded that his understanding of this introduction to Hyperstudio was helped via the cooperative learning process.[12]

By observing the children, Peter learned how to differentiate his communicative approach with the different children. In addition to eliciting other students' help, as he states above, he also learned how to modify his own communication. He wrote:

> I documented that "sometimes less is better." I had explained keywords in several different ways. Andrew dealt with any explanation that I gave him. Luis and Marji, I observed, were served better by explanations that were short and direct.

He was learning how to scaffold, what Bruner[13] describes as taking steps "to reduce the degrees of freedom (less is better) in carrying out some tasks so that the child can concentrate on the difficult skill she is in the process of acquiring."

More importantly, Peter was learning how to create spaces that respected what the children brought with them to the school. Peter wrote:

Allowing the students to write and speak in Spanish from time to time provided me with an opportunity to show my respect for their culture and native language. Having them explain final products in English assured me that they understood the program and were continuing their development in the English language.

From the observations, the professional articles read, and the discussion with these two teachers around the children being observed, Peter was also able to engage in new ways of teaching and of reflecting on his teaching.

To introduce Hyperstudio, the computer program the children would be using for their writing projects, 16 keywords or phrases were identified. Students were to count 16 blank cards where they were to copy the keywords or phrases. The stack of cards was placed in an individual folder with the student's name on it. These 16 index cards were to be used when engaged in a Hyperstudio project in the classroom or in the lab. About this part of the process, Peter reflected that:

> Writing the words on index cards, placing the index cards in a stack, and storing the index cards in a project folder created a direct manipulative (hands-on) analogy to our Hyperstudio computer program projects. For example, cards are stacked, projects are created, and these are stored in folders in the Hyperstudio program.

Peter was learning different ways to scaffold the language for the children. He made overhead transparencies of the 16 keywords and phrases for the children to have available as he introduced each one, explained, and demonstrated them. Later he added visuals, clip art, for each one of the words or phrases. When he introduced and demonstrated what each of the words or phrases meant, he had a microphone. The children later used the microphone, overhead projector, and presentation techniques to teach other students in cooperative group formats and to do presentations for book talks and poetry nights, which were photographed and videotaped. Peter used the strategies he learned in this setting with other groups of teachers and students. About his learning with respect to the technology, Peter states:

> One need look no further than the children's faces for proof that this increases student interest. Looking into the future, my desire is to tie computers and the curriculum together with respect to the New York

City writing standards and to aid our students in their attempt to meet and surpass these writing standards.

I included this example for two reasons. Often, monolingual teachers do not know how to deal with the bilingual child. Peter did not either, but was open to learn from those teachers who were more prepared to do so and who were also willing to put their knowledge to test through inquiry. This integration of bilingual and monolingual teachers in professional development projects around bilingual children needs to be encouraged, as this case illustrates.

Peter told me that he was learning English-as-a-second-language strategies; that he was learning how to scaffold the child's learning. He repeated how excited he was whenever I met him in the hallway or at a school event. When I examined what he wrote in his portfolio, I realized that he had learned a lot more. He was learning to understand the language systems the children brought with them into the lab; how to respect, value, and use what they brought as resources for his own teaching and their learning; and how to balance this with his own need to know that the children were indeed progressing in ways that he wanted them to and that he could help them learn—through English.

ACTIVITIES

1. Take an already existing unit of study for the grade level you plan to teach. Think through how you would like to incorporate the culture of the child in the unit and develop one lesson more fully by identifying resources (Internet, books, film, etc.) that would assist you in doing this.
2. If you have a classroom experiment with a mixed-language group permit them to respond to each other in either of the languages. Share what you found with your classmates.

ENDNOTES

1. I was invited by Professor Joyce E. King, Benjamin E. Mays Chair and Professor of Educational Policy Studies, Georgia State University, to submit a lesson and participate in an online discussion. I, in turn, invited Isabel Fletcha to provide me with a curriculum she had developed so that we could analyze.
2. The children's literature in this unit were Seuss, Dr. *Green Eggs and Ham*. (London: Collins, 2002.); Falwell, Cathryn. *Feast for 10*. (New York: Clarion Books, 1993); Soto, Gary, and Ed Martinez. *Too many Tamales*. (New York: Putnam, 1993).

3.   Banks, J. "Multicultural Education: For Freedom's Sake." *Educational Leadership*, 49, 4 (1991/1992): 32–36.

4.   Coerr, Eleanor. *Sadako and the Thousand Paper Cranes.* (New York: Penguin Group, 2004).

5.   Torres-Guzmán, Maria E. *D&D Initiative: PS165 Second Year Report 1999/2000*, available at: www.alliance.brown.edu/dnd/DnD_Reports/PS165_Report_1999-2000.pdf (2006). Last access February 28, 2009.

6.   Bialystok, Ellen. *Bilingualism in Development: Language, Literacy, and Cognition.* (New York: Cambridge University Press, 2001, p. 136).

7.   Perera, Hilda, and Marina Soiane. *Kike, a Young Cuban Refugee.* (Minneapolis, MN: Tutleback Books, 1998).

8.   All children's names are pseudonyms.

9.   Grosean, François. *Life with Two Languages: An Introduction to Bilingualism.* (Cambridge, MA: Harvard University Press, 2d ed., 1998, p. 18).

10.   Id.

11.   Alzaldua, Gloria. *Borderlands/ La Frontera: The New Mestiza.* (San Francisco, CA: Aunt Lute Books, 3rd, ed., 2007, p. 81).

12.   This is Peter's perception of the efficacy of what he did. I understand the limitations of such an assertion with the evidence provided. Nonetheless, this was his first move in the direction of adjusting instruction so as to be more inclusive of the children who did not speak English. In subsequent years he continued the use of the "keywords" as the words that have the most potential for unlocking meaning.

13.   Bruner, Jerome S. *Actual Minds, Possible Worlds.* (Cambridge, MA: Harvard University Press, 1986, p. 19).

PART THREE

INTELLECTUAL DEVELOPMENT
AS FREEDOM

8

TEACHERS SPEAK
THEIR THEORIES AND EDUCATIONAL GOALS

ↀ

In this chapter, I discuss what teachers of the school said they learned when we asked them to identify spaces of professional development at PS 165 during Ruth's tenure. In other words, we asked them to reflect on their teaching as learning. We wanted to know not only what pushed their learning but also what they learned.[1] While most of the time I worked with a cadre of volunteer teachers, in this chapter, I rely on a broader sample of teacher voices. It is a representative sample of all the teachers in the school. The sample includes teachers from the monolingual regular education, dual-language education, and special education (mono- and bilingual).[2] We conducted interviews of teachers who had been in the school since Ruth arrived as principal and another set of teachers that came into the school midway through her tenure. The interviews were conducted just a month or two after Ruth retired.

I relied on a recursive and recurrent qualitative analysis[3]—the reading and rereading of these interviews. Initially, I used the categories we had jointly selected with a research group that included the interim principal and teachers—administration, evaluation, testing, enhancement programs, and staff development. The teachers were free from any allegiance to any particular administration. The assistant principal became the interim principal after Ruth retired, and a search for a new principal was going on. I felt that the situation had shifted for the teachers. As the school moved out of the threat of being taken over by the state, the teachers had been freer to develop their thinking as teachers. The interviews would give them the opportunity to exercise their intellectual freedom and to be critical thinkers about their profession and its goals.

The teachers' voices were not homogeneous; they reflected a school that was still in development. The voices, as one would expect, were multiple. Thus, I try to keep the variety in thinking I found within the reporting of the results of the interviews. It is not my intention to give the reader a list of beliefs, values, and wants, as I would have to provide as many lists as there were teachers. What I want to do in this chapter is to portray the more fundamental issues that were captured through the interviews during that one moment in the history of the school—I want to give a sense of where the teachers were in their intellectual development after Ruth retired.

As I muddled through the interviews for the umpteenth time, the questions emerging from the conversation were far beyond what I had ever imagined. The teachers conceptualized what they had to do in terms of their academic and social goals. The goals of self-empowerment, independence, interdependence, and social justice were deeply held. The evidence was articulated in the interviews when Ruth retired from the school.

What I understood was that the teachers were not extraordinary in their search for new ways of teaching; they were quite ordinary. Many schools in many places have teachers engaged in similar searches and are acting on what they know even though they do not verbalize or articulate it in the same way. While the teachers are ordinary in the above manner, they are also extraordinary in that they were engaged in an ongoing pursuit to do their work each day better than the previous day even when they did not know how to frame what they had been doing in any sophisticated or elegant way. The sophistication or elegance came through their search.

In their desire to solidify language equity institutionally, beyond the dual-language education, and within a context of freedom to pursue issues of social justice, they were now conversing about the relationships between their self-empowerment, dependence/independence, interdependence, and social justice. Now, I will turn to what they were saying and explore potential meanings of these issues.

EMPOWERMENT

When the teachers spoke about empowerment, they spoke about their process as teachers. Empowerment, in this context, is the ability to be in touch with the constraints—lack of knowledge; way of being; temporal, physical, or social space; materials, etc.—that inhibit the learner's ability to construct his or her identity as a learner other than that which has traditionally been assigned to him or her. If the gist of what has been said by others is interpreted by the learner as "being dumb," whether that was exactly what was said or not, the learner will construct his or her being as a learner as "dumb." For many adults, and most children, what holds them back may be a fear of embracing a new identity. Fear can block us from stretching and embracing our full capabilities. Environments that remove the obstacles to the possibility of being fully open and free to learning are necessary to move the learner beyond where they have traditionally seen themselves. An empowering environment exists when it can remove the obstacles that hold the learner back. The learner can then choose to step into a new way of being—a learner engaged in the empowering act of thinking. Ruth's administration dealt with the constraints teachers faced that impeded them from being the best teachers for the children of the school. Ruth once told me:

> Where people within the school saw constraints, I had to deal with it and remove them.... I had to tell the school personnel, "Tell me what you need to do a great job—what time, what money, what do you need?" I saw myself as the facilitator for that growth. Leadership is to give room for others to explore and explode intellectually. I did not see restrains where other people see them, and I still don't."

The teachers were conscious of Ruth's effort. "I think the administration was very effective at the beginning to encourage us to become involved with one another. So once that was established, we took it upon ourselves to take our relationship to another level, to where it is now, where we can provide that emotional, professional support." This was one of the teachers' responses.

The teacher also verbalized where in the process the support was important—at the beginning. She also verbalized the choice and self-initiation necessary for empowerment to occur. Teachers had to support each other through establishing relationships that would help achieve empowerment.

Another teacher spoke to how the administration supported teachers on an ongoing basis during the year. She said,

> [The administration goes] through the entire year's scheduled activities and if we are interested in attending a specific workshop, we just notify Ms. A or Ms. B so that ... they can hire a substitute and we can go and attend that workshop ... the entire day. So, in terms of that scheduling, they're very supportive in providing those opportunities to have professional development. In terms of the mentoring program, they were very supportive in that as well. Providing the opportunity for someone to come into my classroom and cover me while I would go to another classroom and observe Ms. E or Ms. F, and vice-versa. If they wanted to come into my room and observe, the administration provided the person to cover them for those 45, 50 minutes ... as well as providing common preps for us to meet and have discussions around our observation. On Mondays, we have a common fifth-grade prep, so there we take up any issues that we want to talk about as a group. Once a month we meet with Ms. I, she was working with us in terms of nonfiction. We would meet at 12:10 to talk about nonfiction. As well as other issues that we might have for that matter and so forth, we would have that common period. It's available if you need it. It's not always used for meetings, but it's available.

The teachers' conceptualization of empowerment was not just about the kind of environment that was set up; they spoke about their own agency and the role they had in the self-empowerment process. Stepping into their spaces of work in this way, their proposals pushed their thinking. One of the teachers put it this way:

> I have always been a researcher. I have been always open to new ideas.... They are exciting to me. It is exciting to read books on the latest research about spelling; about phonic ... my house is stacked with books, how-to books of all kinds. On how to make things, how to make projects, portfolios. I belong to the book club of Scholastic. I spend a lot of money on books and games. I have about 30 CDs for elementary teaching—the entire "how to's," the critters, Shiela, and all those things that have games.... As I told you before, it is the teacher that has to empower herself.

I think it is important that the teacher saw herself as having an "open mind" and "empowering herself." She spoke to having the self-confidence to seek out assistance through reading and trying out different materials and methods on her own. The environment was an asset to her learning and development. Not all teachers were as self-sufficient as this one. Many needed assistance from others. For example, the following teacher, while squarely identifying the motivating force as children, she sought out assistance from other teachers.

> What pushes me is when I see children needing help and I do not know how to help them. That is when I particularly like asking teachers about ideas and strategies. That pushes me, when I see a child and I cannot meet their needs. I will ask someone.

Despite the difference in the source of their self-empowerment, the teachers anchored their motivation to learn and develop in the service of the education of the children with which they work. They set up environments in their classrooms; they spoke about doing so to create freedoms for all the students—through both independence for the individual and interdependence among students. This was how they conceptualized contributing, in turn, to the empowerment of the children.

INDEPENDENCE

I became intrigued by the teachers' conceptualization of their goals as I came to understand how the teachers positioned themselves in the spirit of developing the children intellectually and socially. While there was no specific item in the interview on these issues, they continuously came up when speaking about teaching.

The teachers did not speak to the relationship between language and cognitive development directly; instead they spoke about independence as referring to two interrelated domains—the intellectual and social. They suggested that the children's intellectual and social developments were connected. This relationship came through when they spoke about their struggles to build the social organizations of their classrooms. They wanted to set up environments to assist the development of the students' knowledge, skills, and attitudes. Moreover, the learning environment had to engage the students in learning by themselves, independently, or with their fellow classmates. In other words, the teachers' reflection of setting up classroom environments for learning was associated with students' self-sufficiency and autonomy as learners. How some of the teachers set up learning environments, however, reflected their experiences. One of the teachers told us:

I structure my classroom to give more independent work. I think people came up with the idea that it is better to assign group work, but I don't think it always works. I think there is always a kid that can really do it, a couple of kids who are really confident, and a couple of kids who get lost in the process. So, in this, I agree with the standards now. I agree it is necessary to require that each kid be accountable. I think it is a good idea to have all kids write, instead of assigning certain kids to do other than writing jobs. In the group, there might be a stronger writer or a kid that can't write. A kid that really cannot do it, you know. I could take the nonwriter into consideration, but in a group of four there would still be three kids that would be sitting, waiting, while one kid is writing. I think that is ridiculous. Everyone should be accountable in that situation. Yes, they have jobs that they all have to complete. But, what I find functions well with this group of kids, because each group is different, its pair work. They listen to each other and they give each other the chance to say their thing. They each come up to work individually with me and are accountable in the same light. Each of them is accountable for their work.

I found much that I could question when I came to what this teacher said. I could see she may not have had preparation in the methods of group work that would help her see the value of groups in practice. She was obviously conceptualizing writing narrowly. Her perspective of writing seemed to be one in which the writer is the one who puts marks on a paper to create text. She was not considering the possibility of writing as thinking and other members of the group providing ideas for the scribe. What she is most reasonably concerned about is whether the individuals are pushed to their fullest in the relationship of social organization to accountability. Despite all of this, what I think was important was that she connected the students' independence to the social organization she set up.

There were other points of view on how to help the children in developing independence. Independence, in the following excerpt, is in relation to the teacher. The teacher spoke to us about pushing the individual to do work, even if the way to get there required work with others. Her focus was on the preparation of students for group and pair work. She stated:

I think they work pretty well in co-op groups [by the Spring], but we spend a great deal of time at the beginning of the year on what should go on in a group and what occurs in a talk, and we get a lot of practice as a whole group. When we have group talks or other types of talks, they watch my questioning; they watch what I'm doing and what I'm saying. I ask them to watch me in my conferences with them and with others. It is not until January when I really start to expect them to be able to be in a group and be independent. Mainly because they need time to watch what goes on, discover—what does she say to me when she comes over to talk to me about my writing? How does she tell me to spell a word if I don't know how to spell it? So, when they go with a partner or when they go with a group and they say, I don't know what to write about, they're sounding more like what I say. The subsequent question is, what are you an expert on? What do you know a lot about? They can say: "I know a lot about dinosaurs."

The teacher described various aspects of the process—opportunities of observation, practice, imitating the modeling, discovering and establishing the language, the roles and the relationships required—in order for the children to be comfortable in making the activity their own. She talked about how development of this sort takes time.

Another teacher mentioned another aspect of social organization in creating an environment for the children to internalize relationships of independence that permit them to learn and develop. She said:

Groups of kids you work with, depending on the sort of internal structures they have, dictate the kind of classroom you can have. Those internal structures have to be considered in the classroom and have to be placed in the classroom from the beginning so the children learn how to use them. It dictates the way you teach. If you want to have a more open setting, where kids are roaming and independent workers, that is fine, but it has to be taught early on.... They need to get the scaffolding until they can work independently. We are talking about academically, emotionally, and socially. Can kids handle the independence? Some kids cannot. But, it definitely dictates the type of tone and relationships I have in the class. That has been a realization.

The dynamics of the group of children and their internalization of the rules in the classroom are important for how teachers teach. It is not just about the different groups at different grade levels; the teachers spoke about the relationships between students and the internalization of the academic work. One of the teachers told us:

I do not think I could get the work I got out of the kids if I did not give them the scaffolding; this year's group in particular. Last year's group was more independent and of higher functioning academically. This year's group needed that kind of scaffolding, and in the end that makes them more independent. If the kids do not show results in the beginning and you do not help them, by the end of the year they are not independent.

The nature of the instructional activity and the connections the teachers make with the children—their interests, their motivations, and their identities—is another factor they mentioned. The following teacher spoke to her responsibility for creating innovative ways of reaching the students so that they would connect with the curriculum. In other words, her perceived challenge as a teacher was to create an environment that helped the child see himself or herself implicated in the act of learning. She said:

I'm really about reaching my kids. I'm really attentive to building innovative, rigorous work that excites children into learning. I have high expectations for them. I really want to see them being able to love literature, really having them connect to who they are, and what they are about. I want them connecting that to academics. I do so giving them an English-rich environment that still uses the skills and strategies they learned in Spanish.

Finally, one of the teachers spoke to the role of the teacher and his or her responsibility to the social group. She spoke about the social relationships between the teachers and the students and how these relationships must be grounded in respect and responsibility. In the following excerpt her proposal has an influence on developing social and academic independence in children.

I think if you respect kids, they respect you back. I think you give them the responsibility and they want to come back and hear, "You're responsible." I think kids need to be told a lot of things and I think it is about their social development. I think if you give them the tools, teach them how to talk to each other, because some kids don't know how to establish academic talk[4] and they need the tools so they figure it out by themselves. And you have to teach them how to read and write, be responsible, social, and civil with each other. In other words, you give them the tools to be responsible. Then the kids are more reflective and, hopefully, will learn how to solve problems. I give the kids these tools, but every aspect of the child's development has to be dealt with early on in the year in the classroom. We talk to each other; we solve problems together. A lot of times we do self-evaluating or group evaluations, you know, "What's wrong with the group?" and "What do you think we could do differently?" I am trying to give them the tools so that they can say, "Alright, now I can do this on my own."

Independence of learners, as teachers propose, is a critical educational conversation. The teachers implicate themselves in the progress of their students in becoming independent when they connect it to how they set up the learning environment in their classrooms.[5] They spoke about two types of independence—social independence and intellectual independence—as they were connected and needed to be seen in this way.

INTERDEPENDENCE

The issue of social relationships within the classroom environment necessarily led the conversation to the issues of interdependence in the classroom.

In the following passages, the teachers talk about how they established environments that were dynamic, and how, in time, they were able to see how the school changes occurred in their own classrooms. They attend to how social norms within a given classroom, group, or partnership were developed. One of the teachers focused on the change in roles over time, confirming the interrelationship between roles:

I would say that over the years, I really have seen the switch in the roles students play in my class.... Years ago, I was the teacher with the sole responsibility for imparting knowledge and do all the teaching, and ... talking, in the classroom. Right now, I am more or less a facilitator that guides the students to explore and discover themselves, their concepts, and their knowledge. The students are much more responsible for their own leaning now because they have projects that involve research, involve writing and reading, and that they have to present by certain due dates.

With her new role as facilitator and the new instructional activity in the form of projects, she proposed to help create greater independence among students. Another teacher voiced the same kind of transformation in the students. She attributed some of the changes to how she proposed students deal with options and choices.

It's about telling someone else, "Well, what about you trying to develop this for yourself. Let's see how that plays out. Then, if you feel that you're not moving anywhere, then what is the next thing you can do?" And, so they did. They went and they resolved it as a group. So instead of me going and trying to resolve it for them, putting it back on them so they could try and resolve it worked. I think that role has been what has changed. Now, we are focused on how can they resolve conflicts themselves. "What are the choices you can make without me interfering?

The other side of students assuming greater responsibility for their learning and stepping into a new identity and role as a learner is the newfound dependence of teachers on students and on their fellow teachers.

I think the role of my kids has changed, in the sense of my relationship with my team teacher.... They have become more active in taking control of the curriculum, where they drive the curriculum, where they provide their own ideas about a specific subject that we're studying. They are basically driving the curriculum. They are the ones who have a choice of what they learn. We provide the parameters, and they get to choose within those parameters what they bring to the classroom, how they share, and how they contribute. In that sense, the role of the student has changed.

There is interdependence among children, between bilingual and monolingual classrooms and teachers, between regular teachers and resource room teachers, between content teachers and language teachers, between the identities of teachers and students, and between the identities of teachers. One of the teachers told us the following:

I think I definitely provide support to Ms. D because we spend so much time together that we are always conversing about how to become better teachers, whether it be from the standpoint of curriculum, disciplining students, or planning. We do a variety of things. Our relationship, at least professionally, we support each other very well.

The conversation about interdependence reminded me of Vygotsky's concept of zone of proximal development (ZPD). He defines ZPD as "the difference between the level of solved tasks that can be performed with adult guidance and help and the level of independently solved tasks."[6] It is a place where the learner depends on the assistance of others in order to push learning to yet another level. It is where the "other," be it an individual or a group, listens, questions, affirms, clarifies, or repeats what the learner is trying to communicate. It is in the act of doing so, that the other—teacher, teacher's aid, student teacher, or classmate (or the imagined other, as in the intended recipient of a letter or an email or the reader of a text)—assists the learner in making sense; in clarifying; in naming; or in figuring out what was physically, emotionally, or mentally unclear at one time. It is the series of acts of social interdependence in the act of learning. It is where both the learning and teaching take place.

As Tharp and Gallimore[7] would put it, it is the place of assisted facilitation. When the teachers talked about interdependence, they meant the tapping into, or development of, social and interpersonal skills that would permit a group of individuals to engage in the act of learning; in other words, the social space for bringing into being what has also been called a learning community, where both teacher and students, and students amongst themselves, deconstruct and reconstruct knowledge. In the previous quotes, some of these elements of interdependence were visible precisely because learning is social, while at the same time that which is being created belongs to the individual. It is both social and individual.

As its nature is social, setting up learning environments also required that the teachers speak to the issues of social justice and language equity.

SOCIAL JUSTICE

Social justice, within, refers to the ability to create new learning relationships that free the learner from the constraints of past history. In other words, the reality of poverty, sickness, race, ethnicity, and linguistic makeup that an individual carries into relationships in his or her school world conjures up dominant beliefs about what that individual's abilities are, whether from the perspective of those in power or the perspective of the need for acquiescence of the oppressed. To set up environments where there is social justice, the process as well as the outcome must be able to enable and demonstrate that learners become independent in learning and thinking as well. The environment must provide the learner with the ability to develop his or her full capacity to engage with others in learning. It must provide a variety of ways for the learners to do so. It must be able to lift human and material constraints that keep them from being fully open to learning. In addition, it must be able to permit the learner to creatively step into new ways of understanding his or her world, in dialogue with others, and free from past ingrained and social beliefs.

At PS 165, the articulation of social justice was primarily in terms of linguistic and cultural diversity and the issues of equity as these describe the salient social issues in the school. As one of the teachers spoke about her work life at PS 165, she said:

> I can't imagine working in a community that was not diverse. I wouldn't even know how to act in a community that wasn't diverse. I do believe that all the kids are capable of anything that anybody in any school is capable of doing. I don't have the language struggle that maybe the dual-language program does. My kids do speak English. They may not speak it correctly, they may not speak it after they leave me, but I don't have to struggle with that. I cannot imagine not being in an ethnically diverse classroom. I have had this year children from Korea, India, the Caribbean Islands—the Spanish-speaking, Trinidad, Jamaica, and the like—African American children. The whole gamut.... I prefer to teach in that environment.... I prefer to be in an ethnically diverse group. It affects me because I feel that that's the group that I could give the most to and it may be because of my own ethnicity that I prefer to do that. But, it's also the kids that I think that I can identify with. I just think that's the world we live in. We live in a diverse world and I'd rather see a diverse world around me and work with a diverse group of kids.

To work in a world of diversity was part of their sense of social justice. Many chose to work with this school and this group of learners. This was a central belief Ruth struggled with at the beginning of her tenure, and at her retirement this formulation was in the discourse of the teachers. They required a lot of themselves. One of the teachers defined her role in making sure that she was responding to all the children in her classroom.

> I teach in English, but they learn Spanish and other languages. I always work with all the students I have. I like to teach them about their heritage, their culture, whatever the group. I try to choose carefully when we study the group. For example, this week, I celebrated *el 5 de mayo* and there are Mexican kids. I have a child from Yemen, and the parents help me out. Last year, I did Chinese, Japanese, and other group cultures. At the end of the year, we had a performance where we danced for the superintendent.

It is not just about cultures and languages; it's about creating community with the children and their families. Another teacher told us about how she made community with the children and their families. She stated:

> We have a sense of community. One helps the other, and they get together and sometimes there are some misunderstandings. Kids are not perfect. And, we have some that misbehave. I call them; I talk to them. "No sweetie.... Listen to me, here. You are my friend. What did your mother send you over here for? When you grow up, what do you want to do? Do you want a good job? Do you want to go to Santo Domingo and buy a house?" Then, I talk to them like a little family. I talk to their parents, too. When I do this, the parents help me a lot. The minute that I create a friendship with the parent, that's it. I had one, a very tough kid who had a lot of problems in the lunchroom. I talked to the mother, she's a beautician. The boy was going to fail. He has changed. He really listened. We have some kids that are not well taken care of. The parents are not scholars like in other schools in the district. They are not composers of Broadway, or musicians. None of that stuff. I wish you knew some of the problems the kids have. They are very tough problems. I work with parents. I talk to them. Mostly, I work with the kids since I know their culture. I'm not from Santo Domingo, but I am Latina. I talk to them about things of the area, I talk to them about when they go back to Santo Domingo and they are on the farm with their grandfather, who has *caballos,* horses. The child knows that I know a bit about his background and the environment he lives in, and that I will have these in mind. I'm not going to spite him because he's Hispanic or minority. He knows this.

One of the veteran teachers spoke about creating community and what this meant over time.

> Yes, I will have sons of theirs and I get to know the community better and the community gets to know me better. It helps my reputation amongst that community and it helps also with what they know about learning and what you do in your teaching goes home and you want it to reflect both ways. You want your teaching to reflect the home and you want the home to reflect in your teaching. So that really helps.

It is not always rosy. Teachers and children also need to be encouraged in the struggle to learn, to develop, and to help others.

> Sometimes it's an uphill battle, all the way around and no one can say. "Oh, great job!" And, I'm not looking for "Oh, great job, great job!"

On the other had, I need you to be my identity, like my kids need me to be their identity constantly. I need to know what's up.

Despite the difficulties, there is a commitment to make sure that the spirit of social justice and language equity are available to all involved,

My main goal was to get the job done in an equitable manner to meet the needs of kids. I mean that was my main goal. When I looked for support it was support for helping me bring some resolution to something I had to attend to, so that I could meet the needs of the kids and other teachers, too. You must understand the culture of this school. You know the main goal. You know that they will help me align my philosophy with the philosophy of the school.

REFLECTIONS ON TEACHERS' PRACTICES AND THINKING

As I reflected on the chapters on intellectual development as freedom, I realized that the teachers themselves had developed to the point in which their curiosities led them to understanding the relationship between language and learning, and the social nature of this relationship. PS 165 teachers had been, for the six years of Ruth's administration, developing as teachers, trying to understand their role in advancing the social, language, and academic development for the children. They explored who they were and how this had a bearing on the students' development.

What I saw, ultimately, was that when given the time to think, the teachers rose to the task and focused on deeply significant issues in education as they occurred in their classroom. Teachers must not be bound; they need not only the autonomy to adjust curriculum to the students they teach, they also need the guidance and support to engage freely in the systematic understanding of their task as teachers. Teachers need to be free to experiment and to reflect on their practices. Teachers need help in doing away with obstacles in their path. Again, I am not talking about unbridled freedom; teachers have to be responsible to the children and the community that they serve as well as to each other.

Another realization was related to how the teachers thought and acted to bring fairness to the situation of the non-English speaking.

The teachers were advocates for these children; they struggled to ensure language equity in their classrooms. Yet, while they were persistent in their stance, the world around them was moving increasingly towards a world of stricter imposition of curriculum and of standardized testing in the name of equity. These teachers, the children, the community, and the school had to respond to the mandates of the No Child Left Behind Act, the 9/11 aftermaths, an entire reorganization of the New York City schools, new school leadership, and the school system's new approach to diverse cultural and linguistic communities. The latter was particularly important because, as is the case nationally, the conservative forces do not see the need for the instructional environment to afford the non-English-speaking bilingual children the choice to use their own native language as a resource for their intellectual development.

Ruth's retirement raised new questions. Could the teachers sustain the ethos of collaboration and development so as to push themselves further to gain greater understanding of the issues that they were beginning to explore? How long could the teachers sustain themselves, particularly if they did not find administrative support? Furthermore, how could they begin to spread what they knew in ways that would inspire others to rethink themselves and their schools so that the spirit of freedom and social justice could come to life? How was this going to be possible when our nation was curtailing social programs and social freedoms?

ACTIVITIES

1. Interview teachers who have been teaching culturally and linguistically diverse children for five years or more. If you do not know anyone at a school near you, you might try corresponding with a teacher from a program highlighted on the Internet as serving similar populations. Ask the teacher about the issues of social and academic learning in relation to independence and interdependence in his or her classroom. Did the teacher always think this way or has his or her thinking developed through time? What pushed him or her to think this way?

2. Each one of us defines social justice issues within our own specific context. Interview three classmates to find out how they define social justice. Compare their definition with the definition within.

ENDNOTES

1. The question does not suppose that learning in unidirectional. When individuals are in a process of development they not only have to learn and grow, sometimes they have to unlearn and clear the slate, so to speak, so that they can develop.

2. The Documentation & Dissemination (D&D) initiative team interviewed 30 teachers in the school; I was able to secure 17 audiotapes but have notes on the impressions of the interviewers for almost all the interviews. In addition, we collected a one page written retrospective of the spaces that pushed their learning. I was part of the D&D team and deliberately chose to interview teachers with which I had not closely worked to prevent contaminating the interviews with my bias in the data collection stage.

3. I used a computer program, NVivo, for the tedious aspects of coding, analyzing, and reanalyzing the data. My graduate assistants and I coded the data first based on the originally agreed-upon codes (the teachers and researchers involved) but after reading and rereading them, we recoded them based on the emerging themes to which I speak in this chapter.

4. The references to "academic talk" were abundant but not all teachers were meaning the same thing. This kind of reference to academic talk came from both the work in second-language acquisition that they were reading at the time, as presented in Gibbons, Pauline. *Learning to Learn in a Second Language.* (Portsmouth, NH: Heinemann, 1993) and the school's participation with Lucy Calkins in the Reading and Writing Project.

5. Dewey, John. *The Child and the Curriculum: The School and Society.* (Chicago: University of Chicago Press, 1968).

6. Vygotsky, cited in Hedegaard, Mariane. "The Zone of Proximal Development as Basis for Instruction," in Luis Moll (ed.) *Vygotsky and Education: Instructional Implications and Applications of Sociohistorical Psychology.* (New York: Cambridge University Press, 1990, pp. 349–371).

7. Tharp, Roland, and Ronald Gallimore. "Assisting Teacher Performance Through the ZED: A Case study," in Roland Tharp and Ronald Gallimore (eds.), *Rousing Minds to Life: Teaching, Learning, and Schooling in a Social Context* (Cambridge, UK: Cambridge University Press, 1988).

9

OTHER THEORIES OF DEVELOPMENT AS FREEDOM

My thinking about what occurred at PS 165 led me to consider the role freedom plays in the life of a teacher. Specifically, I was interested in a teacher who is struggling to set up environments that provide the bilingual learner (and all learners) with the capabilities for engaging in intellectual freedom.[1] This interest led me to explore how freedoms that people enjoy, what Sen[2] calls development, could actually help explain how a school went from one threatened to be taken over by the state to one where an ivy-league university/school partnership flourished.

My interest was not solely in the process by which teachers conceived freedom in dialogue and action with each other. The process was only one aspect. I was interested in what teachers thought about regarding the relationships between teaching and learning, freedom, and the presence of more than one language in the everyday lives of their students. I was interested in their plurality; their capability of going beyond what is, the given, and looking at self, and the world, for what it could be.[3] This ability to be and be otherwise is what sustained the teachers in their struggle for social justice and language equity for the children they taught. The teachers were able to understand that the way they developed the dual-language education program had to provide the bilingual learner with the capability of participating in instruction freely through the use of the two language systems. The program had to adjust the learning environment to make available to the children the resources for expanding their natural curiosities to more systematic understandings of whatever they were learning and to imagine themselves otherwise. Many of the teachers came to this understanding by engaging in inquiry on their own teaching. They realized that the nature of their work involved also understanding issues of independence, dependence, interdependence, empowerment, and language equity as social justice. It was a process of rigorously engaging in systematic understandings of teaching, engaging critically, and acting on what they understood with their views on what could be; it was about the teachers themselves being intellectually free to become critical thinkers.

DEFINITIONS OF FREEDOM

In a country, and at a time, where freedom has come to have many meanings, I stand with the distinctions between positive and negative freedom that Maxine Greene makes. Negative freedom symbiotically connects with the unbridled individualism that is against any kind of social intervention—"I can do whatever I want when I want and no one can say anything." I do not believe this type of freedom is possible or desirable. Positive freedom, on the other hand, occurs when an individual takes on the joy and responsibilities of being personally realized within the context of a social group with which he or she shares values.[4] I believe in this as the ultimate form of freedom.

The distinction between positive and negative freedom brings to the foreground the relationship of the individual to his or her world, which is usually posed as a dualism, as an either/or. Thus, I turned to a critical sociocultural theory, because within its framework the relationship between what is social and what is individual is most clearly articulated. The theory proposes that rather than looking at phenomena like freedom through "bipolar" or the "vertical" lenses, we think about them as having more than one possible center and more than one layer at work at any given point.[5] By doing so, we can look at how freedom and constraints show up in our everyday lives and we can examine how individual and social levels intertwine.

Individual development, thus, cannot be seen as separate from the historical and sociocultural features of the society in which the development takes place. Individual development becomes social as it is performed by the individual and mediated by interactions with others. The contexts are the social institutions—family, school, workplace—of our times and our country.

Unbridled or negative freedom is a culturally and socially constructed naïve way of looking at freedoms within the United States. Moyers[6] proposes that this unbridled freedom is tied to the way we have constructed the right "to accumulate wealth without social or democratic responsibilities and the license to buy the political system right from under everyone else, so that democracy no longer has the ability to hold capitalism accountable for the good of the whole." Sen, in the economic arena, Moyers in the political arena, and Greene in the philosophical and educational arenas, propose that rather than freedom being a private value it is a social one; it is both a gift and a legacy that reminds us of the memories of struggles others have waged; it is a social responsibility.

THE INDIVIDUAL AND SOCIETY

In the literature on freedoms, one finds the relationship between the individual and the community has been framed as a dualism, as two independent phenomena that rarely meet or are in conflict. Some time ago, Dewey[7] traced the historical role of the individual and the collective in relation to freedom and education. While acknowledging the Greeks' historical importance with respect to the concept of democracy and freedom, he proposed that their specific construction of these concepts was reflective of their society. Coloring their conceptualization of freedom was their class-based prism. Freedom was for citizens, not for slaves. A few centuries later, Rousseau proposed a conception of freedom and education in his novel, *Emile*.[8] Rousseau proposed an individualistic conception of freedom. An individual is free in his or her most natural state. There is no role for the nation-state, or the collective, within this conception of freedom. It is with the Hegelian eighteenth-century conception of individual freedom that freedom becomes anchored in the nation-state. Here is where the more modern view of democracy and freedoms emerged. Dewey proposed that the either/or juxtaposition of the individual and society was an incorrect way of posing the problem. Instead, he felt it was more important to emphasize the interaction between freedoms and different aspects of our sociocultural lives. He opened the way to a more postmodern, pragmatic way of conceptualizing freedoms.

I agree with Dewey, in that he defined freedom as a social construction, a social contract. It reflects the historical and cultural times. As a society, today, we are debating freedoms, nationally and globally. On the one hand, there is the pursuit of unbridled freedom of the markets in a global economy in which the gap between our world's very rich and very poor seems to be ever expanding. On the other, there are those who advocate for the unlimited possibilities we can enjoy if we give greater importance to attending to the substantive, instrumental, and basic freedoms that can influence the quality of our lives.[9]

Both Freire and Sen, in treatises on freedom,[10] extend Dewey's analysis to our era of globalization by positioning the individual within the context of globalization as anchored in his or her local setting and the exigencies of such. Their conceptualizations go beyond the nation-state, as we know it today. Freedom is constructed and reconstructed at every single moment in which humans are confronted with a variety of aspects of life. It is an everyday affair. An individual can personally realize his or her freedoms in an ongoing way and within a very specific local context while at the same time addressing much broader and even global issues.

AGENCY

Throughout the book, I have proposed that my understanding of freedoms comes from the understanding that it is personally realized within the subjectivities of the individual.[11] In other words, the individual takes the stance of freedom with respect to not only the choices a situation offers but goes beyond to imagine new choices within the situation. This is true of each of the teachers, the administrators, and—ultimately—the students of PS 165. The individual act is also a social act in that the individual is a social being. His or her existence as a teacher is who he or she is in the moment and all that makes up his or her upbringing, subjectivities—institutional and social contexts.

The individual embodies and redefines freedoms in the act of freedom. Freedom, thus, is not abstract. It is anchored in the individual and his or her subjectivities and the act defining the individual's freedom exists within a time and a community. It is localized.

Its localization, however, does not limit its significance. The importance of the act of freedom can be private; it may not be of significance to any other individual but the person in the act, as is the case of choosing to read one of two novels or of buying X or Y product, offered to the market by the same conglomerate, when we are in the role of consumer. In other cases, however, an individual act can be of great social significance. For example, when Rosa Parks[12] decided to sit in the front of the bus, she stood as an individual in a localized act of freedom, whether she was connected or not to a larger social network promoting such acts of civil disobedience. The significance of this act was that it called attention to a social form of oppression and it spurred a struggle for social freedoms for others.

Agency distinguishes the private from the social significance of acts of freedom and the negative from the positive. Agency is not just an act of individual freedom; it is an exercise of action or power on behalf of self *and* others.[13]

FREEDOM AS PRODUCT AND PROCESS

Various scholars[14] distinguish freedom as both a process and an end. I found this distinction important, as it helped me analyze how freedoms occur in everyday activities as individuals and collectives make decisions and act within educational institutions. It also made me aware of the need to account for the systematic deprivation of opportunities, poverty, inadequate shelter, lack of health care, a drug-infested community, and the like, that both the community and the school personnel at PS 165 faced. Understanding them as unfreedoms helped unveil the personal and social circumstances that led to past decisions and actions by the PS 165 personnel and the need for the transformation to engage in futuristic visions. In understanding the process of freedom itself as a developmental process, I could turn with a surer foot to investigate freedom as a social outcome: To what extent were the policies and practices in PS 165 enhancing freedom? Where was this occurring?

HOW THE SOCIAL FREEDOMS CAME TOGETHER

We live in a time when schools are increasingly strapped by the testing industry as national policies, such as the No Child Left Behind Act, force schools to push their academic curriculum more and more towards what is measurable knowledge. It is a time in which the majority of teachers experience the inability to do much else, other than teach to a past, that which has already been learned[15] and materialized in tests. It converges with a popular discourse where citizens make, correct or not, connections between immigration, economic decline, and multiple languages. It all becomes one package. It is a time when some citizens are, thus, calling for curtailing the use of the native language in instruction—legally in California, Arizona, and Massachusetts and in practice.

In the midst of these strong social forces, the individual teachers at PS 165 acted as individuals and as a group. They brought about change in their local environments. In doing so, they promoted the expansion of freedoms for themselves and for the entire school. Within we have seen teachers engaged in freedom to adjust the curriculum, to push themselves to improve and develop, to experiment, to participate, to voice, to reflect, to do away with fears of lack of institutional support, to be creative and professionally autonomous, and to provide linguistic freedom for their students. Thus, the different freedoms came into being as teachers dynamically defined and redefined oppressions, injustices, constraints, or obstacles that were encountered. The different types of developments were connected and interacted; none may have been the same without the others. What they illustrate is that as individuals, we personify our freedoms in relation to what we perceive and experience as our oppressions. Below, we will recapitulate the three types of development I chose to highlight as the interpretative framework of what happened at PS 165 and what I perceived as relationships between the manifestations of freedoms.

LANGUAGE DEVELOPMENT AS FREEDOM

Language was important because it was through the teachers' voicing that they gave meaning and named injustices, oppressions, neglect, unfairness, and the like. Language as a social tool—the naming and consciousness it implies—is critical. It is in the process of identifying our oppressions that we can choose to surpass what we know to create a new possibility in the future. Because the situation of PS 165 was unique and particular, within its sociocultural context, so were their constructions of freedom. In other words, the stance an individual takes is both bounded by his or her subjectivities and vast in its possibilities. It suggests that the expressions of freedom can be endless.

Not long ago, I heard what was touted as a scientifically based presentation on bilingual children's learning. The focus was on academic language. The presentation was thoughtful in suggesting that academic achievement issues are partially the result of what schools do and that not ensuring that bilingual children develop competency in academic language—as opposed to solely focusing on social language—is an issue schools can tackle. The distinction between social and academic language has taken time for many educators to understand; but here was an instance in which there was some understanding of this distinction. However, in listening to the presentation, I kept going back to how academic language was defined. Academic language was presented as vocabulary development and grammar, and I felt the definition was too narrow. For the first time, I could see how it smacked of dualism, and that it seemed to be based on the Vygotskian use of scientific and spontaneous concepts. Vygotsky[16] proposed that scientific concepts are those that originate in the structured and specialized activity of the classroom and that impose on children very logically defined concepts. The spontaneous concepts of children are based on their experiences on a day-to-day basis as part of living. The Goodmans[17] suggest that these two types of experiences are not as clear-cut as Vygotsky proposed. They give the example of the work on funds of knowledge to substantiate their point. The funds of knowledge[18] proposes that what is known through the home and community can potentially become intellectual resources for classrooms. In some ways, Dewey's and Freire's[19] proposal that it is not the experience itself, but how we think about the experience that creates the possibility of knowing resonates with the funds of knowledge work. Moll, Gonzalez, Mercado, and other scholars show how the information they gather from homes and communities can be brought into classrooms and the curricula. In other words, the concepts of everyday life can be transformed into scientific concepts, and the scientific conceptual development, ultimately, must be in the service of everyday life. How a child transforms his or her everyday understanding into scientific conceptual understandings and how he or she applies scientific conceptual understandings to the everyday situations is the real test of independent thinking.

I have made reference to the distinction between ingenuous and epistemological curiosities, and the relationship between the two. It is also a dualism unless what we focus on is the process. Ingenuous curiosity is exemplified in the type of questions we raise naturally as part of an experience. An example would be: What makes a ship sink? This question may come from the sinking of a toy boat in the bathtub, from seeing a film about the *Titanic*, or from reading or hearing fishermen's stories. The paths that lead to questions leading to conceptual knowledge can be varied. The inquiries we could engage in and around issues related to ingenuous questions can be endless. In the case of the sinking ship, we could discuss the concepts of mass, volume, buoyancy, and the like.

We could engage in the systematic study of the incidence of sinking ships as a literary device. This systematic engagement in inquiry and the thinking emerging from it is what leads to understanding the nature of the object of study. The latter is what Freire[20] called epistemological curiosity; but it is a process of the connections between the two, and the process must necessarily be multifaceted and multidirectional.

Referring back to the presentation on academic language, I was also reminded of Bialystok's work[21] in which she proposes that learning is more than lexicon or grammar. She proposes that it is more like a system constituted by communication and learning. It is a process of learning about relationships and meanings. Learning language includes what we know and how we use language, how language and culture play together and play on themselves, and how cognition and language dance until they embrace in the creation of knowledge, just to name a few. This kind of knowing about the complexity of language requires the engagement of the learner in the learning as well as the study of the language. Thus, by separating the languages for instruction, as was done at PS 165, the teachers were permitting the students to develop the two systems that they already recognized cognitively, and they were learning to use the two systems socially in conscious and unconscious ways. It permitted the learner to engage in inquiry activity through which the distinctly codified knowledge legacies could be accessed. From Bialystok's work, as well as that of others, we could differ with the presenter. The narrow, linguistic grammar as a scientific way of knowing was not the only thing bilingual children needed to know. What they need to know is much more. Let us go to the research on the differences between bilingual and monolingual children to speculate about what bilingual children need in order to develop their understanding and knowledge of the world, including that of schools.

One of the differences is related to language functions. There is a range of differences between speakers of one language, if we look at functions. To begin with, let me say that even the dualism of mono-lingual and bilingual can also be challenged, but that is not the task at the moment. There are as many types of monolinguals and bilinguals as there are children, and within we are temporarily holding them constant as a way of exploring what differences might exist because differences are seen in classrooms. I do so instead of sweeping under the rug the differences or instead of stating that all children are the same, as my belief is that we have to take what we know about bilingual language development and use it to push bilingual children in appropriate ways.

One piece we are pretty sure of is that both bilingual and monolingual children share in similar processes of language development. Yet, research also documents how bilingual children develop differently in a linguistic sense—at levels of phonemic awareness, lexicon, and cognitively. Let's take a look from the perspective of what might be obvious from a classroom teachers' perspective.

A teacher can distinguish between the bilingual and monolingual children in the classroom. The bilingual child's heightened phonemic awareness shows up in the swiftness with which he or she catches errors of pronunciation, or as we saw in Rebecca's lesson, how the students caught the orthographical error. A child's pattern of heightened awareness and quick thinking is often ignored, because teachers do not always have the opportunity to engage in a more rigorous and systematic study about the use of multiple languages in classrooms. Therefore, teachers stay at the ingenuous questions and responses to their students' needs. They focus on mispronunciations or difficulties in stabilizing a pronunciation or on the bilingual learners' struggle to get the two phonemic systems right.

An example of a two-year-old trilingual in French, Spanish, and English, my own granddaughter, brought this issue up clearly on a Christmas visit. Amelie was having difficulty with the English pronunciation of "h," as in the words "hot" and "hurt." She pronounced them as "urt" and "ot." She could hear the different sounds; she just could not produce them yet. I heard her mother drill some of the words, but to no avail. The drill practice was not bad, because Amelie still needed to hear the correct sounds. This did not mean, however, that she could produce the sound on demand. In our conversations later on, both her mother and I agreed that Amelie was still working some of these sounds out in her childish trilingual reality. We concluded that there was no reason to be concerned about her development.

The words children use in their speech is another way in which teachers can differentiate between student groups. While bilingual listeners may hear the choice of their words as logical and, to some of us, as powerfully spoken, it may not sound quite right from a native speaker's perspective. I always find Amy Tan's[22] writing full of images and associations that do not sound like something a native English speaker would use. Yet, her skill in using nonnative images makes her writing stand out. Word choice is slightly different for the bilingual children because their social contexts call for them to respond by using the different linguistic systems. About this, Bialystok writes:

Monolingual children are more wedded to the familiar meanings of words than are their bilingual peers. It is as though the meaning is inherent in the word, an immutable property of it. In contrast, bilingual children are more willing to accept that the meaning of a word is more convention than necessity, more agreement than truth. We are free to break the agreement if we so choose.[23]

Research indicates that the growth in bilingual children's vocabulary during early childhood is numerically similar to that of monolingual children. What is different is that the actual words belong to different linguistic systems, thus making the vocabulary in each of the languages for the bilingual child less than their monolingual counterparts. Yet bilingual children eventually catch up, but much depends on the sociocultural context and learning environment. No wonder it takes time for tests to be able to measure what bilinguals know.

It has been relatively easy for teachers to identify the code-switching capabilities and uses of bilingual students in classrooms. I have had a few beginning teachers investigate the use of code-switching in learning as master's degree projects, and there are quite a few studies on code-switching because the switching between and among languages is a very distinguishable phenomenon among those who know more than one language. Grojean calls this capacity an "underlying linguistic competence that permits ... movement along the dimension from bilingual to monolingual modes indicat[ing] that linguistic representation[s] for bilinguals [are] importantly different from that of monolinguals."[24]

What is perhaps less well-known and articulated among teachers is the distinction between the linguistic and cognitive processes of monolingual and bilingual children that underlies the proposal that a strong theoretical foundation is essential for a pedagogy that is based on the separation of languages and language equity. What is operating for the bilingual child can be linked to the fact that he or she attends to two linguistic systems simultaneously. Bialystok found that the bilingual child is able to restrict his or her thoughts about language, in general, in such way that he or she can entertain more than one alternative to a specific linguistic and social situation. She asked the bilingual and monolingual children to demonstrate that a printed task could have more than one meaning. The bilingual children consistently showed their superiority on this task. She summarized the research as showing that there is "a bilingual advantage if processing occurs as a function of an interaction between demands for representational analysis and demands for attentional control."[25] What she means is that there seems to be an earlier appearance of control over the higher-order cognitive processes among bilinguals. She identified the cognitive process as attention and inhibition in relation to the two language systems. The presence of the two systems, in order words, requires that the bilingual pay attention to the systems of both languages, and in order to distinguish between the languages, the bilingual has to be able to put aside, or inhibit, what he or she knows in one system in order to work with the other. This finding, however, does not mean that bilinguals can engage in abstract reasoning better than monolinguals. The cognitive processes are many. She does suggest, and I agree, that the higher-order skills available as a resource for bilingual children might carry over in other domains if formal educational settings can use them as resources to facilitate learning and development. Her findings support the necessity for various forms of enriching the education of new language learners. Bialystok states:

> The social context requires different solutions for different kinds of children. It is certainly not necessary to provide bilingual education for all children from all backgrounds, but the data clearly demonstrate its benefits for children who need the supportive environment and linguistic structure that are part of a bilingual class. This had been shown for both learning English and keeping their own language. Educational programs must incorporate at least some of the diversity reflected by the children they are designed to serve.[26]

Thus, bilinguals use the two systems for learning whether they are supported or not in the classroom. In a comparative way, we can state that an English-only classroom environment is an unfreedom for the bilingual learner as he or she is not supported to access his or her learning in the most powerful and effective way possible. The schools may not be able to push for the most powerful bilingual learning modes that would constitute freedom for the child, but certainly they ought to be pushing for as much freedom as possible, because only then can they make a claim of doing right by these children. Only then do they have a chance of measuring what bilingual children can do with greater validity.

INTELLECTUAL DEVELOPMENT AS FREEDOM

Schools, like PS 165, are the designated social institution, aside from families and some would say media, providing the young in our societies the focused space to develop their human and social capabilities. This makes them very important for the development of individual and social capabilities, including bilingualism. This was an important aspect of the educational work at PS 165. It is through human signs and symbols, particularly through language, that we internalize the social and the cultural. Schools are as important as homes (and media) in mediating social and cultural understandings. They facilitate the children's conceptions of justice and propriety that, in turn, influence the specific uses that young people make of their freedoms.

Hostos, Dewey, and Freire, as well as others, dealt with the process of freedom and what makes learning possible. Hostos and Dewey[27] proposed the distinction between knowledge and thought as critical to understanding learning. Learning is not just the acquisition of knowledge handed down to us but the connections the learner makes between the knowledge that is transmitted with his or her own reality. It is the back and forth between the ingenuous and the systematic that we spoke about above. Learning is thinking—it is about how the learner goes beyond what is presented and how he or she negotiates meaning within the context of his or her reality. What is transmitted in schools, in sociocultural theory, is in the act of mediation and facilitation of everyday and scientific concepts within the proximal zone of development. Freire[28] proposed that what the learner brings to every situation is an understanding based on his or her own reality, which generates questions of curiosity (what Vygotsky calls spontaneous concepts) that can be submitted to a systematic, disciplined process (which can take on many forms) through which learning can emerge. It is in the latter process, which Freire calls epistemological curiosity, where intellectual understandings take place and new knowledge is created. In Vygotskian terms, it is not just a mental representation of the external but also a new level of behavior—a conceptual development that was once previously possible only with the help of others. Learning takes place when not only the transmitted knowledge (scientific concepts) converges with the learner's reality (spontaneous knowledge) but when the process yields to inquiry. Distancing oneself through inquiry offers the learner better understanding of concepts, permits the learner to make concept his or hers, and creates possibilities of using these learned concepts to mediate new ones. Freire[29] maintains that individuals engaged in epistemological curiosity have the potential of understanding its importance when they understand their own human incompleteness—no matter where we are and how much we know, we still have more to learn and develop. It is in the realization that we are incomplete that the role we have in the making of our future arises. The different educational thinkers push on the dynamism of the process. The incompleteness of our being, as Friere proposes, is the kernel that fosters both critique and possibility of agency, that is, the ability to act and bring about change for self and for others, the ability to transform what is learned and understood in the creation of new possibilities for being.[30]

I often hear teachers say they believe in the ability of all children to learn, and this is true because humans are born, unless some disability impedes them, with the capacities to develop, but that they need a context that assists them in that development and that some children need different environments to push their learning to their potential. So long as we measure children's potential with standardized tests and do not provide adequate environments these constraints will show up as inequities.

PROFESSIONAL DEVELOPMENT AS FREEDOM

What I concluded upon examining PS 165 is that what was driving the teachers was not just self, but concerns of a social nature. They were worried about being able to ensure linguistic equity and social justice. Thus, the process started with a belief in the need for institutional freedoms to use the native language of the children, Spanish, and the need to ensure that this freedom was not going to be sabotaged.

At PS 165, the teachers, administrators, and other support personnel involved converged in their belief that language and thought were intimately connected. The presence of two languages did not alter the nature of this connection. Instead, it sharpened the nature of the relationship and brought new elements to it. It was understood that not only do children use language development for conceptual development[31] but that bilingual children had two language system resources available to them.[32] The languages, and all the resources available within each of the language systems, are important to bring out in more transparent ways in learning situations.

Ruth's perspective on affirming language and culture and academic rigor had a theoretical grounding. The dual-language education program used the two language systems as mediums for instruction so that children could continue to access both linguistic systems as their resources for communication.

The model of dual-language education at PS 165 also contributed organizationally because it separated the languages so that the cognitive processing strengths the children brought with them were more fully utilized in the learning process, not just for speaking about spontaneous everyday concepts but for more abstract learning, such as in literacy and content area learning. Strengthening the two languages in separate spaces provided the bilingual child the freedom to choose from his or her available resources and thus ensured that he or she had greater access to learning academically. The school personnel believed the children had to learn how to play with language in sophisticated ways and demonstrate what they knew in modes of language, including creative expressions beyond oral and print forms of language. That was what Ruth and the teachers called academic rigor. In other words, it is a learning environment based on understanding the complexity of the relationship between culture, language, and learning.

In addition, the learning environment recognized that the native language was the means by which the children found their initial self-expression and the capability of reflecting on and creating a world they could value. The value of language was central to some of the teachers at the school prior to Ruth's arrival and yet there was a tolerance for the unfreedoms faced by the school's student population and their communities. This occurs in many places, perhaps because teachers do not have the space or time to deconstruct the relationships between language, poverty, and education and do not receive the support for developing capabilities to ensure that they, and subsequently their students, are pushed to their full capacity.

It was in the pushing, through various forms of professional development, that PS 165 teachers developed their own capabilities. They had to make this individual development of importance to the development of the children and their community. In order to do this, the teachers needed to know how to make learning occur through curriculum planning and in the enactment of instructional strategies that assisted the children in their learning, what Tharp and Barth call assisted facilitation. The teachers needed to know how to create appropriate learning environments, or zones of proximal development[33] where they could apply, interpret, gain perspective, and gain a sense of the essence of transferability of knowledge and the creation of new knowledge or understanding[34] for bilingual children.

The teachers' concern with expanding the resources for bilingual children's learning required that their conception of academic rigor shift. It was not just an issue of language and learning knowledge, it was also related to thinking and taking ownership of what was being learned. It was the basis for intellectual freedom. Taking children from what emerges as a natural curiosity to systematic study of the object is about developing academically rigor. It also has to provide freedom for the learners to engage in a range of language functions within each of the language systems available to them, as well as a range of language functions that come with the knowledge of more than one language. It is not just creating environments in which the students can experiment with the movement from one language to another; the environment also has to promote expansion of intellectual freedoms. The teachers were striving for freedom of thinking, freedom of language use, and freedom to pursue the questioning that comes naturally when one can freely think about what is and imagine what could be. They were simultaneously struggling for individual children, within the context of their dual-language education program and for understanding how to make social justice and freedoms in the school, in general, occur.

ACTIVITIES

1. Develop a lesson for students at a specific grade level. The objective is to teach your students what agency means, as defined within, and to create an environment of agency within your classroom community. Before you try the lesson, share it with other adults and ask them to assist you in sharpening the different aspects of it from the perspective of what students might have to do to achieve the goal of the lesson.

2. Interview three teachers to find out whether they believe they have instructional spaces in which they feel free to teach their students. Listen carefully to find out how they define the freedoms and the constraints they face. Now that you have heard their perceived circumstances, think of yourself as their principal. Develop a plan to support them so that they can go beyond what is to what could be.

ENDNOTES

1. Dewey, John. *Freedom and Culture*. (Amherst, NY: Prometheus Books, 1989); Freire, Paulo. *Pedagogy of Freedom: Ethics, Democracy, and Civic Courage*. (Lanham, MD: Rowman and Littlefield, 2001).

2. Sen, Amartya. *Development as Freedom*. (New York: Random House, 1999).

3. Greene, Maxine. *The Dialectic of Freedom*. (New York: Teachers College Press, 1988).

4. Id.

5. Garcia Canclini, Nestor. *Hybrid Cultures: Strategies for Entering and Leaving Modernity*. (Minneapolis, MN: University of Minnesota Press, 1995).

6. Moyers, William (Bill), "For America's Sake." *The Nation*, January 5, 2007, p. 14.7.Dewey, *Freedom and Culture*.

8. Rousseau, Jean-Jacques. *Emile*. (North Clarendon, VT: Tuttle Publishing, 1993).

9. Sen, *Development as Freedom*; Raskin, Marcus, and Robert Spero. *The Four Freedoms Under Siege: The Clear and Present Danger from Our National Security State*. (Westport CT: Praeger Publishers, 2007).

10. Freire, *Pedagogy of Freedom*; Sen, *Development as Freedom*.

11. Greene, *The Dialectics of Freedom*.

12. Rosa Parks's connection with the Civil Rights movement was sanitized into a version of her story as just being too tired to stand or to walk to the back of the bus, but she had been an active member of the NAACP, had worked in voter registration, and had been a participant of the Highlander Folk School. Her action was not just freedom individually realized; it was social and historical, with all the subjectivities of her circumstances.

13. Sen, *Development as Freedom*.

14. Dewey, *Freedom and Culture*; Sen, *Development as Freedom*: Nussbaum, Martha C. *Women and Human Development: The Capabilities Approach*. (Cambridge, UK: Cambridge University Press, 2000).

15. Goodman, Yetta M. and Kenneth S. Goodman, "Vygotsky in a Whole Language Perspective" in Luis Moll, (ed.), *Vygotsky and Education: Instructional Implications and Applications of Sociohistorical Psychology*. (Cambridge, UK: Cambridge University Press, 1990).

16. Vygotsky, Lev. *Thought and Language*. (Cambridge, MA: MIT Press, 1962).

17. Goodman and Goodman, "Vygotsky in a Whole Language Perspective."

18. Moll, Luis, Cathy Amanti, Deborah Neff, and Norma Gonzalez. "Funds of Knowledge for Teaching: Using a Qualitative Approach to Connect Homes and Classrooms," in Norma E. Gonzalez, Luis C. Moll, and Cathy Amanti (eds.), *Funds of Knowledge*. (New York: Routledge Publishers, 2004, pp. 71–88).

19. Dewey, *Freedom and Culture*.

20. Friere, *Pedagogy of Freedom*.

21. Bialystok, Ellen. *Bilingualism in Development: Language, Literacy, and Cognition*. (Cambridge, UK: Cambridge University Press, 2001).

22. Tan, Amy, *The Joy Luck Club*. (New York: Penguin Books, 1989, reprint 2006).

23. Bialystok, *Bilingualism in Development*, 136.

24. Id. at 58.

25. Id. at 214.

26. Id. at 239.

27. Eugenio Maria de Hostos (1839–1903) was a Puerto Rican educator, philosopher, political scientist, and humanist who, like John Dewey, raised questions about learning and thinking in the context of the reigning ideologies. His collected works include more than 50 books. He is included in Palmer, Joy A., *Fifty Major Thinkers in Education: From Piaget to the Present Day.* (New York: Routledge Publishers, 2001); Dewey, John. *The Way We Think.* (Boston: Dover Publications, 1997).

28. Freire, *Pedagogy of Freedom.*

29. Id.

30. Sen, *Development as Freedom*; Freire, *Pedagogy of Freedom*; Greene, *The Dialectics of Freedom*; Vygotsky, *Language and Thought.*

31. Vygotsky, *Language and Thought.*

32. Grosjean, F. *Living with Two Languages.* (Cambridge, MA: Harvard University Press, 1982); Bialystok, *Bilingualism in Development.*

33. Tharp, Roland G., and Ronald Gallimore. *The Instructional Conversation: Teaching and Learning in Social Activity.* (Research Report #2, National Center for Research on Diversity and Second Language Learning. Santa Cruz, CA: University of California, 1991). Vygotsky, *Language and Thought.*

34. Wiggins, Grant, and Jay McTighe. *Understanding by Design.* Expanded 2d ed. (Alexandria, VA: Association for Supervision and Curriculum Design, 2005).

10

ONE PRINCIPAL'S PERSPECTIVE

In this chapter, I offer a transcription of the interview conducted with Ruth after I had written all the other chapters in this book. It represents the continuous dialogue between Ruth Swinney and myself. She has moved on in her life and so have I, yet this book has provided us one more occasion for reflection about what happened at PS 165 during her tenure as a principal. It is a conversation that occurred after we went over each of the chapters and added a significant part of the telling. The point of view of my telling of the story was, as previously stated, from the point of view of the dual-language education program, and there was a large monolingual program that I barely touch upon. The following was our conversation.

Maria: Now that we have reviewed and edited the previous chapters individually and together, we have established that I saw the school from the perspective of the dual-language education program and that I missed out on some of the holistic vision that you, as principal, had. We have also established that despite these differences, we do agree that the story told through these particular camera lenses served to understand what happened throughout the school. From your perspective, what did I still leave out?

Ruth: I think that one of the important pieces missing is the role of bringing all the arts into PS 165 and how that enriched not only the language but also the culture of children. You tell the story about what you noticed in the environment that you saw when you came to school on the first days of my tenure at PS 165 and what you saw the day I left, but you do not expound on its significance. I believe that the arts played a vital role in enriching the children and the teachers intellectually.

We had programs like the Studio in the School, the Philharmonic, the Hispanic Ballet Theater, and we were also adopted by [the violinist] Midori for two years, and so on. This emphasis on the arts exposed the children to experiences that they would never have had otherwise, and it gave the teachers different camera lenses through which to enrich the children's language. For example, many of the children at PS 165 had never traveled down to 66th Street and, if they did, they did not know what Lincoln Center was. Now not only did they go to listen to the Philharmonic concerts at Lincoln Center, but they were also able to talk about their experiences with Philharmonic musicians.

Maria: Explain the connections you are making here. How did you see the enrichment of the children through the arts?

Ruth: One thing that was very important for the school environment was that children be surrounded by beauty; we had to take them to museums, we had to connect their understanding of the world with art. For example, that if they were studying Mexico in their classroom, the art teacher would focus on the art of Mexico. In that way, the art teacher exposed the children to a vision of Mexico that they otherwise would not have. Critical to transforming the school was changing the gray and depressing hallways to splashes of wonderful art produced by the students themselves. In this way we provided a beautiful school for the children, and their parents.

The theory of multiple intelligences states that some individuals learn visually, others learn interactively, and so forth. We had to expose the children to different art forms, to open their world to different types of music, for example, and offer them different opportunities to learn. We had to expose them to beauty and the language of beauty. Taking your framework of freedom, there was unfreedom in the depressed environment of the school. It was a curtailment of their freedom because they had not been exposed to beauty where other kids in fancy schools are. Those students that had artistic gifts would have never had opportunities to find beauty and possibilities within themselves if they were not exposed. We sent difficult kids to the Arts Studio, for example, and saw how they transformed themselves. Their teachers saw a nonreader and so the children knew what they could not do; what they failed in. The art teacher, on the other hand, saw a wonderful artist and the children were then able to see a wonderful side of themselves that they did not know existed. They found a new way of expressing themselves and could in turn see their own beauty.

Maria: Wow! That is correct and the door example is where I started. Why did I miss that?

Ruth: The painting of the doors was actually something that occurred at the end of my tenure. Like most people, what you missed was understanding the relationship; the value of aesthetics in education. A lot of our kids live in basements, as their families cannot afford homes in Manhattan. Most children from middle-class homes start with rooms full of colors and shapes all around them. They can afford to think about beauty in natural ways. They are also exposed to museums, theaters, and other forms of beauty. Our focus on the place of the arts gave the students from poor homes an even chance (to the extent that this can be done) with those kids that have these opportunities as natural parts of their environment.

Leaving the arts aside, another part that is not reflected in the text is how parents became active participants in the school. The parent stuff has to do with giving the parents opportunities to participate democratically in our institutions.

Maria: Say a little more about what you mean by democratic participation.

Ruth: Well, as you stated, we organized the retreat, the school based committee, which we called SLT. We had to organize it so that the parents could actually attend. It could not be a pro forma committee. In other words, we could not hold it at times when they could not come and then say that parents did not care. Instead, we decided to hold the meetings early in the morning, when parents dropped off kids, even if it meant covering teachers, which was not easy. What we decided was that we would have a community that worked. It used to be that only two to three parents regularly attended, but their involvement increased dramatically to the point where the committee was composed of half parents and half teachers.

Maria: The issue of parent participation is very critical because this is the source of life for any school in a democratic society and often it is ignored. I started my academic career by looking at parental involvement because I agree that unless we have this, in many ways, the schools are not going to reflect what is important to the community they serve, nor are they able to reflect what parents may desire or want for their children's future. I think that the salient issue at PS 165 was how you turn the relationship of home and school on its head, something not frequently documented in stories about poor communities. Rather than asking parents to support the school through fund raising, you propose that schools can help communities in their struggles. Within, a myriad of ways of doing this were reported. There are many more ways of supporting poor and minoritized communities in engaging in freedoms they do not presently enjoy. This would also transform the home-school relationship from the traditional approach of improving their individual skills as parents, as if all that happens to their children is their fault. The approach you took communicated that you understood that there were many problems that they were facing and that the home-school relationship was a two-way street. You helped transform the lopsidedness of the relationship into a more balanced one. It is definitely a different way of seeing how parents and schools can come together. Let's move on to the social rituals, which I included within the text, but would like you expound here? Can you tell me about that?

Ruth: Well, this is how I thought. If you have a vision, that is not enough. You have to set up a strategic plan and put it into effect. So there were things you had to do at PS 165, but at the same time, in order to do them, you had to change the toxic environment that existed. What you had to change were the relationships between teachers and their relationship with the principal. In order to do that, I had to create some social rituals that would allow me to gain the trust of the staff so I could then engage in more difficult moves. For example, having food during our meetings and giving teachers an opportunity to talk to each other before the meeting sent the message that there was something social about the meetings; that all decisions would affect the lives of people and we had to be responsible in what we did. Having a monthly breakfast for teachers where no shoptalk was allowed and where we talked about their interests and their lives allowed them to get to know me and me to know them so that there were less hidden agendas. Sending them cards for their birthdays created bonds between the teachers and me; it created more confidence in our treatment of each other. So, at the same time that I was targeting two ineffective teachers a year, I was setting up social rituals that created community.

Maria: When you talk about strategic plan, what do you mean?

Ruth: In PS 165 I did not discover a new way to revive a dying school, nor was I Mandrake the Magician. I simply worked with the school community to implement a plan of action that they all knew by heart, because they had been writing plans of action since 1989, when the State Education Department first placed the school under review. The ideas were there; the knowledge was there. But, what they needed was the support, clarity of priorities, and structure to implement a sound educational plan for the school, and to define strategic priorities.

In addition to creating social rituals, during my first year at 165, I created a set of strategic priorities, sort of a five-year plan, like the Russians used to do, which changed over time, but which operated like a map—a guide for me. At the beginning, those priorities were more superficial. We did a lot of work on beautifying the school, rugs and plants and bookcases in the hallways, creating lovely environments in the classrooms, throwing out old stuff, I invested a lot of money on rugs and pretty bookcases, and books for the libraries, I wanted to create model classrooms to get teachers motivated. I also felt that my kids deserved a beautiful environment, I wanted them to connect learning with beauty. I aligned that priority, environments, with my walk-throughs, which in layman's terms means what I observed as I walked through the school. I made my observations public and specific, so that teachers knew what I was looking for. I was very disciplined about it. I used my walk-through priorities as a way to communicate my vision for the building.

The transformation of PS 165 is a work that is still in progress after all these years. During my tenure it was the result of a collaborative and often painful process of soul searching involving teachers, parents, students, and administrators. In order to help change the school, we had to redefine our roles as educators, and to question our aims over and over again. Change was not easy. As the school changed, many teachers decided to leave or were gently and not so gently pushed out by me. Turnover was approximately 40 percent of the staff during my tenure at the school.

We also had a schoolwide vision of how kids learn. When I came in, many of the teachers expressed a view of children as a blank slate because of where they came from, so we had to establish a schoolwide vision of how children learned languages through an exposure to the arts and sciences. This opened the door to learning how to read and write and do math, because what was established was that all children could learn by paying attention to the environment and doing away with frontal teaching. To do this we created model classrooms. These model classrooms energized the whole building. I had to think through how it would look and feel during a walk-through, what were the protocols and how to support the vision through the comments that I gave teachers. Part of the vision, as you state within, was the parallel experimenting on my end with different models of supervision. I very clearly understood that the only way to influence change in people was by being very specific. I talked to students when I walked through. I always made sure I would talk to at least three children and very purposefully selected the top, middle, and bottom quartile of the children according to their test scores, because testing was an issue. I looked at their notebooks as well. I would compare my notes on my first visit to the next week's visit. I discussed individual plans with the teachers based on notes I took for each child and ways I believed that could improve or participate more actively. I also looked at the classroom libraries and the leveling of the books, I looked at the charts around the room, and I looked at the instructional planning from the point of view of students and what differentiation there was for the different kids. My first year supervision, as I look back, was superficial, but I gained experience—it helped me reflect and gain a deeper understanding of what was needed. The teachers were not used to this type of supervision, and by the second year I worked two hours with each teacher when I did the walk-through. I was going for greater grade-level consistency. What I looked for each year was established in our end-of-the-year retreat, because that is where the focus was established for the entire school—from classrooms to lunchrooms. My walk-through focus was connected to the vision for curriculum in the building. Before I went into the classroom, I reminded the teachers of what I was going to look at; it was written on our central white board. It was not a secret. The one thing I would like the readers to understand is that I saw the teachers as partners. I had a note pad with me and wrote a note to the teachers before I left the classroom that I placed in the mailbox upon returning to the central office. It was appreciated and considered a positive communication form. If I had not observed anything positive, which did occur, I would not write but have a conversation with the teacher. I would lay down the nonnegotiable and work with the teacher from there.

Maria: I know that you feel that bringing in the TC Reading & Writing Project was also very significant in the transformation of the school. Can you say something about it?

Ruth: The TC Reading & Writing Project made a tremendous difference in the school. It provided a knowledge base in terms of literacy and created a bottom line for what was expected in terms of teaching reading and writing. It also carried with it a notion about how children learned—in interaction with each other and with the teacher. Instead of the teacher standing in front of the class, it forced teachers to do more group work and individualized instruction than they were used to. Furthermore, it promoted collaborative planning among the teachers. We began to see the children learning and a greater degree of collaboration as a result. Even though not all the teachers were on board with the project, there was a solid group of teacher excited about the work and this was enough to create a dynamic of change. Our reason for bringing the staff developers of the project into the school was because we needed to create a common vision in terms of how we taught literacy. Through their classroom demonstrations and their study groups with teachers, they eventually helped the school to develop a consistent methodology based on the belief that all children could learn. Having units of study for reading and writing began to develop consistency of instruction throughout the grade. We also established a pacing schedule for math. Eventually there was a common set of expectations for teachers and children.

Maria: How would you assess how you left the school?

Ruth: When I left, the composition of the school population was the same as when I started. The poverty level remained the same as well. Yet, there was a dramatic difference in terms of the student performance. This meant that the problem was not in the children. Our school is one example of the evidence that the problem is in the teaching, not because the teachers are bad people but because there is bad teaching occurring. The roof had been replaced, the walls were repaired and painted, and the exterior of the building was restored to its old beautiful architectural design. There was a feeling of hope and joy around the building. The school had showed improvement in all other markers that identify success: student and teacher attendance, school tone, parental participation, and student population growth.

There was still a lot of work to be done: the upper grades were much stronger than the lower grades. In my plan, I tackled one grade at a time. I had focused on the third to the fifth grades first as there were tremendous changes needed. Kindergarten to first grade also needed a lot of work. There were teachers who had been there a long time; also the second grade was in transition, as it had new teachers. This was work that the new principal had to do.

In the lower grades, there were still predominant views of deficiency rather than enrichment, and their expectations were not very high. They did a lot more of play and socializing than was necessary. If I could go back, I would do a lot of things differently. One of the things I would have done was work more on the lower grades. I would have also changed some of the allocation of language in the fifth grade. I felt that many children were going into middle schools that did not honor the native language of the children. I would have pushed to get the teachers to agree to 40 percent of the time in Spanish and 60 percent in English. I know it goes against the theory of dual language, but in this case, the fifth-grade curriculum called for students to understand and manipulate English at exponentially different and higher levels in order to prepare them for English-only middle schools. If we had had the option of a dual-language middle school for all the children, I would think differently and would go with what the literature proposes. In the school district, however, there were few middle schools using any Spanish.

Maria: It reminds me of what Rebecca Freeman implies, in her book on *Bilingual Education and Social Change*.[1] She followed up on children from the Oyster Elementary School dual-language program as they went into the middle school and found that the children did have difficulty in the English-only environments. Rebecca implies that dual-language elementary schools are not enough, which is why districts are moving to also create dual-language middle schools as part of their language education offerings. I may not necessarily agree with the change to the 40/60 as I have been more of a purist on this issue over time. This is, perhaps, a different conversation. In closing, I would like to ask you what you thought about the framework of development as freedom, which I used to tell the story of the school.

Ruth: Freedom as development is an interesting perspective. At first, I reacted negatively to it. When I understood what you meant, it made sense—the lack of education curtails poor and minority students' freedoms in many ways. I had never thought about it in those terms. It is, in itself, a freeing perspective. Usually, we think about the factory model, where the principal is in a box, the teachers in another, and kids still in another. We do not think about what goes across. What we did in PS 165 is that we tore down those walls; there were no restrictions. We did away with the old factory of education in the school. That is what you call development as freedom.

ENDNOTE

1. Freeman, Rebecca. *Bilingual Education and Social Change*. (Philadelphia, PA: Multilingual Matters, 1998).

11

MY PERSPECTIVE

✑

You are me. What is it that I see when I look at your round face and brown skin, when I stare into your eyes of enthusiasm, sadness, or discovery? What is it that I hear when you speak the foreign words that I can understand as they move through you? Why can I get your meaning and intensions when others cannot? Why is it that I feel your pain? Why is it? I am not you. Or, am I?[1]

Why do I care about the children who are learning bilingually and about the teachers who are assisting them build bilingual capabilities? Why have I dedicated my adult life—my professional career—to pursuing questions about education and bilingualism? I believe that inquiries we pursue are always about who we are, our identities, and the world that surrounds us. To know about bilingual children, especially those from the working class, is to know about myself. To know about the teachers is to know who I am when I engage so many eyes that stare at me as if I knew something they did not. It is about being conscious of self in the world, to the extent that it is possible, and this knowing is what can, or what has, set me free.

I am bilingual and the road of bilingualism has meant many things. The development of bilingualism in me has been part of my human development. I do not want to compare myself invidiously with others,

I just want to know how knowing about me helps me see others, or the inverse. Is it not the same in some ways?

Using my own childhood as an anchor, what circumstances led me to my bilingualism? The Treaty of Paris, in 1898, reframed Puerto Rico's future. It was booty of war, with Guam and the Philippines. It went from Spain to the United States, and with it came the possibility of bilingualism. In 1917,[2] the United States gave citizenship to Puerto Rico, increasing the possibilities of bilingualism. With the coming of the mighty north were many matrons whose mission in the island was teaching English. After all, Teachers College, Columbia University, tested Puerto Rican children and supported the need for these English teachers because with it, ostensibly, came intelligence.[3] Puerto Ricans were not that bright, they concluded. By that time, slaves from Puerto Rico had escaped the island, entered the United States through Louisiana[4] and other southern states, and moved up through the midwest. Other Puerto Ricans traveled on the *Tiger*[5] directly to the shores of the eastern coast. The movements of people toward the island, its new status in relation to a non-Spanish-speaking nation, and the movements of people toward the mainland set the stage for bilingualism in the population, not just officially.

The new world the free slaves encountered was English speaking—yet another language not their own, not the one they learned at birth, not the one they used to speak to each other, and not the one their masters on the island used. Even if they kept their languages throughout their lifetime, it would be to speak to each other, their families, and to know about the development of those that were their past.[6] The languages they knew were not their future. Not all faced this fate; there were those that saw in the "Mighty North" possibilities of progressive and profitable encounters, and they worked with people that would listen to advance their causes.

The economy, the politics, and the language were all changing. The 1950s was a particularly difficult period. It was the era of industrialization. Many, like my father, were leaving the sugar cane in search for a better life for their families.[7] My uncle had been the adventurous one. He was a contract worker in the Michigan beet fields when my father decided to look north. Although my father was well educated at the time, as he had gone beyond high school and to a business college, the political scene was at a crossroads. It was changing towards greater affiliation with the "Mighty North." My father believed that, given the history of favoritism when political parties changed, he did not have a chance.[8] He resolved to join my uncle and other in-laws in a steel factory in the booming city of Detroit. By then, there was a Puerto Rican governor on the island, and bilingualism in the schools was the norm.[9] No longer was the school taught in English; the political forces and the social realities had pressured the government to move back to teach in Spanish in 1948. English, however, became the children's second language from the first grade onward.

I was born in Puerto Rico during this time. My mother had stayed behind with the children. We arrived in Detroit when I was a year old. Until then, I had only heard Spanish spoken. I began hearing English in my new surroundings. My two older sisters started school a few years later. Our family was Catholic and they sought out the church for support systems. The Mexican community extended Puerto Ricans a hand. The Mexican community had already moved into the Corktown parish church, Most Holy Trinity, on the southwest corner of the downtown area. I remember living in various homes throughout my childhood; all of them were around the Bagley-Trumball area. By the time I was four years old, I wanted to attend school. I must have insisted plenty, as I remember my father taking me to visit various public and private schools. I was too young and rejected by all of them. That made kindergarten at Most Holy Trinity at age five especially exciting.

My elementary schooling, thus, was in English and in a private, Catholic setting. While I still spoke Spanish at home, which we would still do into adulthood, I internalized the English I picked up from children and adults around me, especially my two sisters who were already in school.

In addition to bilingualism, poverty was also my social reality. While I bore what I now know were the unfreedoms of poverty, I did not know them as such. It was what it was and I knew no better. Nonetheless, living in poverty did mark me in how I reacted to situations and what I thought about people. When I was about six or seven, I remember feeling crushed at the loss of a pair of boots that my father had just bought me. When I realized I had left them somewhere, I began crying. I was crying because I would have to forgo the boots and because I had to tell my father. I no longer know if it was that I was afraid of what he would do or if I actually thought about the fact that my father had nothing to show for his effort. I think I must have known (in my body and bones) the scarcity of money. I remember my despair and my tears. While growing up, I have gone back to this memory. One thing I am sure of is that lack of money did not translate to lack of caring, ever. Once the loss was established, my father moved to console me. Then I saw my father as having the biggest heart I could have ever imagined. Instead of scolding me, he made me happy. He bought me what I now imagine was a five-cent doll. For me, it etched a spirit of love, caring, and generosity. My father may have been poor in his ability to purchase because we could not afford another pair of new boots that winter, but he was not poor in spirit.

Multiculturalism was also part of my growing-up experience in Detroit. Not only were Mexicans and other Latinos part of my life; so were the Irish, the Maltese, the Polish, the Hungarians, the Armenians, the Chinese, the African Americans, and the whites from the South. We all gathered around Tiger Stadium; we loved baseball and hotdogs.

Our life took a turn that would be significant for my development as a bilingual person. When I was eleven, my mother and the five children went to Puerto Rico for a visit and stayed. We started school in the local Catholic school, San Ramon Nonato.[10] This time it was the inverse, school was now in Spanish. I do not think I worried much about it because I believed I was smart and I thought I knew Spanish.

Coloring my belief in myself as a learner was the IQ testing in kindergarten. I tested out as a borderline genius. I did not know what it really meant but I knew that those around me were pleased, including my parents. Only as an adult did I learn of the controversies associated with testing and IQs. As a child, I believed I was smart and I got good grades. The point is that at that age I did not blame myself for what I encountered in school in Spanish. Everyone told me that I was sufficiently intelligent and would pick up the language quickly. Even the mother superior of San Ramon Nonato came into class one day and told the teacher, in front of all the class, that my school records had come in and I was very smart; she did not say the same thing about another student who was also new to the school, from the neighboring city, and knew Spanish.

My father had taken time, while in Detroit, to dictate words and have us write them down. I thought I had reasonable command of Spanish. I remember trying to explain what I knew about the Crusades in class, but I recall few understood me. On class dictations, I did horribly. I also had many embarrassing moments around language.

The Spanish I knew when I went to Puerto Rico was the language spoken at home, by my parents and their friends. The circle of Spanish-speaking friends did not consist of solely Puerto Ricans; there were many Mexicans and other Latinos. The Spanish I was learning was not an actual standard of any nation; it was a mix. While my Spanish improved exponentially when I went to Puerto Rico, I remember being fascinated by one of my grandmothers, who would whip up a storm of swear words in Spanish in a second. It was a feisty and spirited language and, as an 11-year-old, I wanted to imitate her. It was a language model that was fun and earthy. I tried it out in different settings until one of my schoolmates gave me a sense of how I was being heard in school, by them—my peers. It sounded too *jibaro*[11](rural Puerto Rican), she told me. Within my family it was a way of speaking, but I was at an age in which what my peers thought mattered. In addition, I was an outsider, a Puerto Rican from Detroit, wanting to belong. I had to speak the part. I did not want to sound too off the mark and I toned down, particularly in the swearing.

As an adolescent and return migrant, I became conscious about the languages in my environment. I remember doing comparative linguistics in my inner world. I thought about the spoken and written language of books. The Spanish of Puerto Rico did not sound as sophisticated, I thought, as the Spanish that I saw in books. The academic language of the books mostly came from Spain, but there were some others from Latin America. Only teachers of Spanish tried to mimic the language of the books. We had to write language that was booklike but we did not have to speak it this way. Actually, if you spoke booklike, you were being pretentious. I also thought the English I was learning in the schools in Puerto Rico as very elementary. After all, it was being taught as a second language, and all of my prior schooling had been in English. In my inner world, I was making the kind of invidious comparisons against which I speak now. What I was actually doing was internalizing variations and hierarchies of the languages in my environment. I was also internalizing the value, and shame, of my bilingualism. I had two worlds to explore. Bilingualism, however, was the marker that differentiated me from other children in both the English-speaking and the Spanish-speaking worlds, and as a child I did not want to be different. The evidence, in my childish mind, was that I was not at par with the norms of Spanish, and I would never be to the academic Spanish in the books. I was also internalizing the colonial relationships of, and the attitudes toward, the languages.

Being bilingual, in my mind, had nothing to do with my smartness. When I had changed from private to public school, my placement was in the smart kids' class. My association with these smart Puerto Ricans, an oxymoron in other people's eyes, would be my reference and foundation. Some of my fellow classmates to this day continue to accompany me in many of my journeys. I just did not know either language as well as what I saw written in books and how I thought I should. I cannot say it did not shake my confidence in my intelligence, though. I did not get great grades initially in Spanish. The traditional dictations were disastrous at the beginning, even though it did not stop me from talking about the Crusades and the Middle Ages (even though I had far to go in my academic language and no one really understood me). Yet, when I misspelled "studying," leaving out the "y," or when I was not sure whether "immediately" was spelled with two "m's" or an "n" and an "m," as in *inmediato* ("immediate" in Spanish), I felt shame. Shame brought silence in my life for a very long time. After I displayed my less-than-perfect pronunciation of a word I read in the eighth-grade social studies class, the roaring laughter of my classmates shamed me into choosing to refuse to speak and display my knowledge in a classroom until I was in graduate school. This did not stop me from creating friendships, it just humbled me in the classroom. I would have other holes in cultural and local knowledge compared to my classmates, and their ugly heads would be unveiled periodically, to my disappointment. Nonetheless, I became comfortable in Spanish. There was never a question about the academic track placement. I got good grades, and the test results were always superb. Most importantly, I could write, and by the time I was a sophomore in high school, I received public recognition for one of my essays. I remember my adolescence as dynamic and fruitful. They were my formative years, and belonging was of great importance to me then.

As a young woman, I was also learning about the relationship between gender and education. I loved math. I did a comparative analysis of the math I was being taught or had been taught in each of the languages as well. In Puerto Rico, I experienced ways of thinking about math that stressed imagery embedded in everyday life. I had learned some theoretical aspects of math in my elementary school in Detroit that proved to be of value within the Puerto Rican setting. I had learned the theorem of the number nine and the conditions under which it did not apply.[12] I did not know why what I knew about the number nine impressed my teacher, but I was encouraged to present what was by that time my theory about the number nine to the local math and science fair. This knowing proved to be valuable, as I received local, districtwide, and regional prizes. With that experience behind me and a high school math female teacher who was shy three credits from her degree in engineering, I started looking into a career in this area. One of the big petroleum multinational corporations in Puerto Rico at the time, CORCO,[13] put these ideas to rest. They discouraged me from pursuing a career in engineering. I went to the career fair and asked them about the possibilities of a scholarship in industrial engineering, and they told me that they did not provide funding for women in the field. I was disappointed, but accepted what they said. The ticket to furthering my education was a scholarship, there was no doubt.

My mother managed to organize diligently and valiantly the education of five children. I knew poverty in a new way as an adolescent. I remember the shame of poverty when I went to the store to buy kerosene for our two-burner top stove. We did not even have a tank outside the house that would periodically have to be refilled! Poverty, however, was not to stop us. My mother had bought a piece of land; we had all pitched in to build a house, and my two older sisters were in college.

My SAT scores were the highest in my school, among the top 3 percent of the island. Therefore, while I had had my heart set on being an engineer like my teacher, the world was open to me. I chose to stay and attended the University of Puerto Rico, Rio Piedras campus. My interest turned to what was happening in the late 1960s in Puerto Rico, in the social sciences and humanities. I was 15 then.

I could not miss the issue of political status in Puerto Rico; it permeates everyone's thinking every day in an existential way. It was in my hometown the first year that I was on the island that I also encountered the reality of Puerto Rico's colonial status. It was the day of John F. Kennedy's assassination. I was not yet aware of what had happened, but the bell for physical education rang and we were about to begin playing. We were just throwing the ball to each other when I heard the physical education teacher saying things I did not understand about *el imperialista yankee* (the yankee imperialist). School dismissal, I thought, left me only with sadness and tears for Kennedy. He had been a man my family had rooted for, as he would be the first Catholic to take such high office within the United States. The latter was the overwhelming feeling then and for some time, but the sting was there. I engaged in my own inquiry. I wanted to know what this teacher was talking about and I eventually would understand the current colonial position Puerto Rico has in its relationship with the United States and the historical relationship with Spain. It would help me understand some factors contributing to how I felt about my bilingualism as a child and why other people's freedom around multilingualism matters to me. It would also lead me to understand another form of freedom that I felt many, including myself, desired—political and economic freedom.

Naming, as Maxine Greene says, is a big part of the process of realizing freedom because it becomes symbolic of the oppressions, hurts, constraints, and injustices one feels.[14] I did not know how to name what I was going through then, but I have learned to claim them as I have engaged in the pain of knowing, the enjoyment of discovery, and the quelling of my thirst for knowledge over the years. I can now name the linguicism,[15] classism, sexism, racism, and colonialism in my life. Not only can I name them, I have understood that I no longer have to be their victim. I wear with pride that which I choose to be. I no longer speak an "illegitimate, a bastard language," as Anzaldua[16] put it. I now advocate not only for others to understand the nature of varieties of Spanish and English, I am an advocate for the freedom to choose to speak multiple languages. I have also learned that we negotiate multiple identities; some are situational and others more enduring and I have also learned that identity is linked to the sociocultural context in which we live.[17] It used to be that land, economic status, and family anchored who we were. Today, ethnicity, culture, language, job status, gender, and personal preferences play more significant roles than in the past. With respect to language, I borrow some of Anzaldua's words to express how I have often felt.

> Ethnic identity is twin skin to linguistic identity—I am my language. Until I can take pride in my language, I cannot take pride in myself ... I cannot accept the legitimacy of myself. Until I am free to write bilingually and to switch codes without having always to translate, while I still have to speak English or Spanish when I would rather speak Spanglish, and as long as I have to accommodate the English speakers rather than having them accommodate me, my tongue will be illegitimate.[18]

I do not recall when exactly it occurred to me, but it was during my adolescence that I came to understand my experience of being bilingual/bicultural as a freedom. There were various types of freedoms that being bilingual offered me. I recall it specifically as a freedom to think and to be. I could escape from the parochialism of knowing only one language, living in one place, knowing one people. I had a real option of going somewhere else. Why not? I came from a different experience. So, it was not just my bilingualism but my cultural experience as well. To love Spanish, Puerto Ricans, and Puerto Rico was one thing. I get much of who I am from there—how I organize myself (sometimes there is much to be desired here), how I go beyond boundaries and expand, how I prioritize the social above other aspects of my life, my laughter and joy, and my sense of social justice. I love this part of me with passion; those who know me know this well. Nevertheless, I also felt its oppression, and it brought me despair, sadness, and powerlessness. I sometimes felt stuck (maybe it was the small-town feeling) and I had a vision of myself in another space.

I did not stay stuck. Most of the time, I was in another space as I read furiously in both languages (I still do, as some things never change). I saw my bilingualism as a freedom to explore my worlds—the real and the imagined. Both English and Spanish had wonderful, rich literatures. As a second or third grader, I was an advanced reader placed in a special reading group with an older nun. Reading in this group is one of my clearest and most enjoyable memories of elementary school.[19] I loved leaving the classroom to take pleasure in reading. I remember staring in delight, focusing on all the nun gave—her facial expression, the spark in her eyes, the tone of her expressions, and the movement of her delicate and shriveled hands as the tunic hung from her elbows. I recall the pride of holding a thick book for the first time. I was going to read this book alone as well as in the group. It was through this reading group that I learned about libraries and what checking out books (literally and figuratively) meant. I do not know if other families did the same, but throughout my childhood I was devout about the trip to the library every two weeks—even when it meant walking in the cold weather with the piercing wind on my face and battling the slush and the snow on the ground. We did not have many books at home, but that was what the library was for—it had hundreds of books through which we could explore the worlds we knew, could imagine, and beyond.

I experienced my bilingualism as a freedom to escape from norms I did not subscribe to, that I opposed, that I did not like, and/or wanted to resist. As a child, I remember my mother imposed those norms. We, the children, would find ways of escaping her rules. One way was speaking in English.

As an adult, I have had many opportunities to escape in my being the "other," which is essentially how many bilinguals are treated in my English-speaking surroundings. I recall that in my first job as an education specialist in a Mexican American institution,[20] I exercised this freedom. While I was a Latina, the immediate indicator of my not belonging to the Mexican American community with which I worked was my language—I spoke funny, not like them. My first informal encounter around linguistic difference with my Chicana colleagues was significant in establishing who was who. I do not know now if I wanted to make the distinction or if I felt the difference swelling as I spoke. In any case, we had gone out to lunch at one of their homes. There was a point where I was telling them about my driving trip from California to San Antonio. I was telling them about my passing through Las Vegas, Nevada, without having gambled one penny. I was proud of myself because at every stop there was a tempting slot machine with the incredible bells chiming as if yelling out, "you may be the lucky one." I expressed my pride by saying the following, "*Pasé por Las Vegas y no me cogió ni un chavo prieto.*" Those of you who know the different meanings must be rolling on the floor by now, as my colleagues did. What I meant and said in Puerto Rican Spanish was, "I drove through Las Vegas and did not leave one cent." What my colleagues heard in their Mexican Spanish was "I drove through Las Vegas and did not screw even a black man." My acknowledgement, self or externally imposed or both, of "not being one of them" was an internal struggle. While I worked to be a part of the organization, not belonging gave me some opportunities to exercise my freedom. I could do things I wanted and could claim I did not know or that I did not traditionally do this or that in the way as expected. At one point, I realized that I did not have to invest myself as if the organization was my destiny. I could disconnect at any point in time. I had the freedom others did not have. It was not about my language itself, but my language was a vehicle through which I experienced this.

I consider myself very fortunate. I do not know what would have happened to me had I stayed in Detroit all my life, but I do know that going to Puerto Rico enriched me. My experiences in Puerto Rico filled me with pride and knowledge about who I was and where I came from. I learned Spanish well enough to do well in all standardized tests and attend undergraduate school, with scholarships, at the University of Puerto Rico in Rio Piedras. I had Puerto Rican role models in all areas of my life. I was rooted in a town, with a set of friends, and with a life to which I still feel a sense of belonging. The self-confidence that comes with a sense of belonging was very important to me. I believe it is also important for the children I have chosen to care about and to which I have dedicated my career life. I am always looking for ways that teachers engage with children that communicates this belonging.

I knew this was important when I returned to Detroit after finishing my undergraduate training in Puerto Rico. Many of my elementary childhood friends had left school, they were married and had a few children; they were only 19 then. It had not crossed their minds that they would ever have a chance to go beyond high school. I asked myself, why did I? I knew I had a mother who had a mantra that education was our ticket out of a bad marriage, but I do not remember my mother being very different from their mothers. Actually, some of them were family. The one big difference I saw was that I had had the opportunity to know and be proud of who I was. I was constantly reminded of who I was and of my history through the media in school and in my everyday life. I had learned to be proud of being Puerto Rican—the entire package, including knowing Spanish well enough to be able to go to school in Spanish.

When I returned to the United States, I had to relearn many things. While in Puerto Rico, for example, I experienced class, not ethnicity, as the driving force that created wedges between people. I would spend many hours discussing with a cousin the reasoning underlying his advocacy for Puerto Rican power. After all, those in power on the island were Puerto Ricans as well. I did not see race as the driving force in Puerto Rico, although in hindsight I could see how this played itself out in the language and behavior of the Puerto Ricans on the island. I had to experience race and ethnicity anew to understand the issues my elementary school classmates had internalized.

The light bulb went off in San Antonio, Texas. I was traveling to Mexico with my husband, and we stopped to see my roommate from my Ann Arbor, Michigan, graduate school days. I had noted the increasing rudeness in treatment that we experienced as we drove south, but I only saw it as rudeness. I came to know how to name it in a gasoline station in south San Antonio, when the attendant would not serve me unless I had the exact change or a credit card. Of course, I had a credit card and gave it to him. At that point, he said that he had to check to see if it was worth more than five dollars, which was what I told him we would approximately need to fill the tank. (What a difference in oil prices!) He responded that he still had to check it out because sometimes credit cards were not good for the money. I was offended and turned to comment with my husband. My then-husband, inexplicably to me, barked back, "You don't know racism when you see it?" I sat there, misunderstood by those around me until I finally understood. Within the United States, many social realities converged in a blinding confusion—it was not just an issue of class, it was ethnicity, racism, and linguicism. It was a complex reality—truly felt, not just imagined.

I could then put some memories of my childhood back on the table to reanalyze. I had just buried some of them as experiences to be silenced. In the fifth grade, my teacher was a nun transferred from New Mexico. Although all the documents were available to her about me, she repeatedly refused to recognize my smartness. By that time, I struggled to be the best student in the class in all the subjects. The nun always put another classmate, a girl who was my friend and competition, before me. This wall was one that was very hard to crack, as she made me feel that she did not believe in me. No matter how hard I tried, I was never good enough. It was after the incident in the Southside of San Antonio that I carefully unlocked my buried chest of pain around racism and understood the nun's chosen discrimination and bias against the Spanish speaking. It did not matter whether the pain came from the color of my skin, the language I spoke at home, or what. It was through the understanding of my experience that I was whole.

It was then that I understood I needed to make sure this did not happen to others. I became active on the Ann Arbor campus and in the Detroit southwest Latino barrio. I became a representative of the group of Puerto Ricans (we were five) at the University of Michigan, at Ann Arbor to the *Unidos* conference in Washington, D.C., in the early 1970s. I participated in the youth group's effort to write resolutions upon which the nation's activist Latinos could unite. Corky Gonzalez,[21] Cesar Chavez,[22] and other political characters of the Latino movement, visited us through the evening and the night. I did not know them, but I remember capturing their symbolism and how it tied to our language and ethnicities.

I went from receiving a master's degree at the University of Michigan to the community struggles in Detroit, Michigan. The Civil Rights movement was contagious, and there was grassroots action all around. I became a faculty member at the now defunct liberal arts Monteith College, at Wayne State University. I also immersed myself in the black and Latino community political struggles of the time. At the university, I pushed for bilingual education to come into being at the School of Education. One of the big issues in the Detroit community was the *Bradley v. Milliken*[23] desegregation case. I volunteered to organize a Latino community response with a local community agency that culminated in an intervention suit of which I was a signatory. It was in this role that I began to understand the legal implication of language of instruction and where I met and/or read about the important voices of the times—Dr. Maria Brisk in Boston and Dr. Isaura Santiago in New York. They were expert witnesses in court cases around the language rights of Puerto Ricans and other Latinos. It was then when I returned to school for a PhD at Stanford University in bilingual education and when language became not just symbolically but intellectually salient for me.

Undertaking a long, rigorous, and systematic examination of the role of language in education is what has led me to writing this book. My activism continued in California, particularly in San Jose, where I lived. I was committed to understand the role of language within the Latino community. This was important to me, as I had sworn that, upon leaving Ann Arbor, I would not return to school unless it was critical to me and that the study was worth it. At Stanford University, as in many places throughout the nation, the study of bilingualism was barely starting. I was amongst one of the first federal Title VII (the 1968 ESEA, Bilingual Education Act) bilingual doctoral fellow recipients[24]; we were ten in total at Stanford. Our cohort of students would have to be pioneers in the field. Of particular importance outside the School of Education was the work of Dr. Eduardo Hernandez-Chavez from the Linguistics Department. That first year of the Title VII Act, I was invited with our Title VII coordinator, Dr. Arturo Pacheco, to attend one of the early national gatherings in Washington, D.C., of Title VII fellows.[25] I was to present what our cohort of fellows thought were research needs in the field. Wow, we had barely met! With one semester under my belt, I was at a loss but excited about being handed a leadership role. I chose to step into it. While I was young, barely 25 years old, I was willing to assume these responsibilities even though I had doubts about being a spokesperson and representative of a group of scholars.

The time at Stanford University was what set the intellectual foundations on language and education that I would later pursue. The class Professor Hernandez-Chavez put together on Chicano Sociolinguistics was priceless. The members of the class were facilitators of and scribes for many presentations of national figures on language. It connected me to an extended academic world.

There were many formidable experiences. Dr. Charles Ferguson[26] called on a group of bilingual student to discuss a sociolinguistics minor in which many of us enrolled. I remember, within the context of one of his courses, studying the role of bilingualism in Puerto Rican history. By doing so, I began to understand more clearly the role of sociocultural and historical contexts in understanding the role of language in colonization and its relationship to political freedom. Bilingualism has to be viewed in context.

My studies in anthropology were critical. Language on its own, even as encased as sociolinguistics, was not a sufficiently satisfying area of work. I needed it to be broader and I need to be grounded. With this later group of scholars, my goal was to understand the relationships between culture and language. I came back full circle to understand that there was more than language in what we say and how we say it. I decided to focus my dissertation inquiry on the importance of community involvement and what happens in schools.

My scholarly work at Michigan State University influenced my work. I went into schools to work collaboratively with colleagues and teachers.[27] Naturally, when I came to Teachers College, Columbia University, my work centered on collaborating with teachers and their learning. I did so with other schools in the district, and PS 165 was the school I stayed with for a while. I still work with them. Here, however, I have looked for my collaboration with colleagues primarily outside the College—with *La Colectiva Intercambio*[28] and with Cultivating New Voices[29] of the National Council of Teachers of English (NCTE). I am still in search of a similar collaboration with colleagues at my own institution.

I have indulged in my own history and for this I ask the reader for forgiveness. I have done so because by examining it I have come to see why the complexity of bi/multilingualism, learning, culture, society, and freedom has been an enigma and area of inquiry that ultimately generated this book. It is when I look into the eyes of the children and the teachers that have made me care about the multilayered and complex relationships that I see my life unfolding. Moreover, I have come to believe that as Sen[30] points out, it is important to understand the interrelationships between different types of freedom in everyday situations if we are to understand how specific freedoms can be put to the service of creating greater freedoms that will better our lives. Within, I have tried to make a case for the need for institutional freedom for educational programs such as the dual-language education program, where the use of the native language of the child is part of the medium of instruction. I do not argue this from the standpoint of language rights but from the standpoint of development as freedom and the need to expand the freedoms that we enjoy as a society. I see this as a possibility and want to engage in conversation with readers about its social value.

I have examined the learning that the cadre of teachers from PS 165 undertook as they encountered the perplexed or excited faces of the children and the difficulties of delivering language equity under a host of societal and institutional constraints. I did so based on my belief that, as the teachers of PS 165 undertook the task of professional development, it was not just to improve themselves but also to ensure that the educational environments that they provided bilingual learners would build their capabilities of engaging in intellectual freedom. The teachers had to find the seeds of freedom for themselves as a way of ensuring freedom for the children. The teachers had to ensure that they were able to instruct in the two languages and that the administration was supporting rather than sabotaging their work. They had to have freedoms within the curriculum to be able to explore the relationships between language and cognitive development, and how to set up environments in their classrooms that would support the intellectual, social, and linguistic development of their bilingual children. The teachers had to understand their role in facilitating and assisting their students to distinguish between the two languages while using both language systems as resources for their intellectual, cognitive, and academic development. Thus, they had to understand the social nature of language and learning and their role in carving out environments that promoted activities where the learner could socially engage in interdependence while intellectually maintaining independence.

To understand what the teachers understood and how they acted on behalf of the children was important for me personally and professionally. Moreover, it was by knowing the role of freedom in language and education that I better understood the institutional and policy-level need to protect the students' rights to the use of their home language to learn in schools and in other social contexts. It meant that not only would the children have the opportunity to learn, they would also later have the opportunity to choose their language. I have come to understand that it is only when, as individuals, we know more than one language adequately that we can truly choose how to express ourselves and in what language in any given situation. It was in knowing more than one world, and associated languages, that I could choose to care for that which gives me life. But the private, individual choice is intimately connected to the social choice.

Furthermore, it meant that I and, for that matter, the teachers, could not accept the way things were going when experiencing increased unfreedoms to use the languages of the children as mediums of instruction. We have to go against the political givens and the surging wave to restrict rather than promote language freedoms. We have to struggle to improve ourselves, and our ability to deliver rigorous instruction, if we are to create new possibilities where there are only closings. We have to make these possibilities real by exercising our responsibility to create the social environment to make it happen.

Given who the children, and their communities, were and the social, political, and economic constraints the school, the administration, and the teachers faced, the teachers saw their work toward language equity as symbolic of their work for social justice. I have come to agree with this. I have also joined the teachers in understanding that one victory in this process is not sufficient. This work has to be undertaken on an ongoing basis and goes well beyond the classroom and school walls.

When I look at you, I see me. Wait, I am not you. Nor are you me. We are individuals and we are unique. I choose to be you freely, as through you I can be in touch with my plurality, my humanity, and my ability to empathize. I can be me. I can be free.

ACTIVITIES

1. Write a narrative of some part of your life. Look for spaces of freedom that were significant in your development. Share with a family member. Ask him or her to think about those experiences in his or her life. What did you learn in doing this exercise?

2. Create a lesson that is based on one of the various freedoms. The first time around think of the context of freedom as permitting someone to do as they please. What do you think will be the result? The second time think of freedom as personal realization. What do you think would be the result? What can you see is different in your thinking as you created the two lessons?

ENDNOTES

1. I did not go through a bilingual program but cannot help but to identify with these children and particularly with those who do not have access to the home language and are left intellectually wanting.

2. The Organic Jones Act of 1917 (renamed the Federal Relations Act) granted Puerto Ricans U.S. citizenship.

3. In 1925, the International Institute of Teachers College, Columbia University, surveyed island schools, finding that more than 80 percent of the school children were dropping out of school. Refer to Kandel, I. L. (ed.), *Educational Yearbook of the International Institute of Teachers College Columbia University. New York, 1925–1944.*

4. After the abolition of slavery in the late 1800s in Puerto Rico, some of the free slaves left the island by joining the trade ships coming through the New Orleans route.

5. The *Tiger* was an English-commanded pirate ship that roamed the Caribbean seas during late sixteenth and early seventeenth centuries. It is said to have carried Puerto Ricans to the area that later became the United States. In *Roanarke,* by Lee Miller (New York: Arcade Publishing, 2001, pp. 83–84), the *Tiger* was documented to have stopped in Puerto Rico from May 11th through the 23rd in 1585.

6. When I worked at Wayne State University, the students did oral histories in the African American community in Detroit where some of the Puerto Rican slaves had settled. Many of them kept their language but they did not pass it on to their children.

7. Sugar, tobacco, and coffee were the agricultural economic base until the turn of the twentieth century. There was a rapid transition to an industrial economy in the 1940s through the 1960s. My father had been a sugar cane worker before he went into the U.S. Army and prior to migrating to the United States, as many others on the island.

8. In Puerto Rico, since the U.S. takeover of the island in 1898, the political parties have been organized around the aspirations of the people in defining the status of the island in relation to the United States. The Republican Union (1930s–1960s), a precursor to the existing New Progressive Party (PNP), which was in favor of Puerto Rico establishing itself as a state within the United States, had won some local elections in the early 1950s.

9. The island had experienced a see-saw (between English and Spanish) period of language policy during the 1898–1948 period of U.S. rule. The first elected governor, Luis Munoz Marin, appointed Mariano Villaronga as the education commissioner of Puerto Rico the same day of his inauguration in 1949, as the issue of language of instruction had been a critical one during the election. Shortly after, Spanish became the language of instruction on the island.

10. El Colegio San Ramon Nonato was the catholic parish school in Juana Diaz, Puerto Rico.

11. *Jibaro* is a term used in Puerto Rico to refer to people from the countryside and mountain areas.

12. My theory of nine was not complicated. It was how I checked my multiplication results. The rule was simply that every answer had to sum up to nine. For example, $9 \times 4 = 36$ and $3 + 6 = 9$. I would play endlessly with numbers to find patterns that would help me remember.

13. The Commonwealth Oil Refining Company (CORCO) of San Antonio had refinery and petrochemical plants in Peñuelas, Puerto Rico, and had a significant presence in the life of the southern part of the island, where my family is from.

14. Private conversation with Maxine Greene (November 1, 2004).

15. Tove Skuttnab-Kangas introduced the concept of linguicism in 1986. She speaks about the concept in her 2000 book, *Linguistic Genocide in Education or Worldwide Diversity and Human Rights?,* published by Lawrence Erlbaum Associates, Mahwah, New Jersey.

16. Anzaldua, Gloria. *Borderlands/La Frontera: The New Mestiza.* (San Francisco: Aunt Lute Books, 3d ed., p. 80).

17. Henry Torres Trueba spoke to situated versus enduring identities in his 1999 book *Latinos Unidos: From Cultural Diversity to Politics of Solidarity.* (Lanham, MD: Rowman and Littlefield).

18. Anzaldua, *Borderlands/La Frontiera,* p. 81

19. Most Holy Trinity Catholic School in Detroit, Michigan.

20. Intercultural Development Research Association (IDRA), an educational consulting firm in San Antonio, Texas

21. Rodolfo "Corky" Gonzalez (1929–2005) was a Chicano political and civil rights activist from Denver, Colorado. He was the author of the epic Chicano movement poem, *I Am Joaquin.*

22. Cesar Chavez (1927–1993) was a farmworker, labor activist, and civil rights leader. He was one of the founders and leader, until his death, of the United Farm Workers. He led the farmworkers' Delano grape strike with the philosophy of nonviolence.

23. The *Bradley v. Milliken* legal case established the schools of Detroit as segregated institutions and ordered desegregation with suburban districts. The intervention suit was the Latino communities' attempt to keep enough students who did not possess sufficient English skills together to establish a bilingual program, given that the laws called for at least 20 students in each grade level. The desegregation case was viewed as a potential interference in making a claim for bilingual education. I was a signatory to the intervention suit along with other community members.

24. Under the Elementary and Secondary Education Act (ESEA) of 1965, the Bilingual Education Act of 1968 was also known then as Title VII. By 1975 the Title VII Fellowship was established. Its purpose was to fund doctoral students in interdisciplinary studies in the field of bilingual education. I was one of ten fellows at Stanford University in 1976.

25. In 1977, the then-project director of the Stanford Title VII Fellowship Project, Paquita Biascochea, visited the campus and, during the meeting, asked to speak to me afterwards. She invite me to go with the Stanford Project Director, Dr. Arturo Pacheco, to Washington to report on what we thought the national research priorities ought to be. Later that year, Professor Pacheco and I attended the Washington Fellows Meeting.

26. Charles Ferguson (1921–1998) was best known for his linguistic work on diglosia and was key to establishing the field of study of language and society.

27. I worked with Frederick Erickson on the project we came to know as Teacher Development and Organizational Change at Michigan State University School of Education (1984–1986).

28. *Colectiva Intercambio* was a national collective of Puerto Rican researchers in the United States and in Puerto Rico that was funded by the Center for Puerto Rican Studies at Hunter College. The main faculty members were Pedro Pedraza and Carmen Mercado from Hunter College, CUNY; Ana Helvia Quntero and Diana Rivera Viera from the University of Puerto Rico; Luis Moll from the University of Arizona, Tucson; and myself.

29. Cultivating New Voices is a project funded by the Research Foundation of the National Council of Teachers of English. Its aim is to support young scholars of color who are either finishing their doctorate or in the beginning stages of their academic careers.

30. Sen, Amartya. *Development of Freedom.* (New York: Random House, 1999).

12

CONCLUSIONS
OPENINGS FOR FUTURE FREEDOMS

꘎

I wanted to finish this book with some thoughts about the sustainabil-
ity and the expansion of freedoms like the ones documented within.
The theory on which I want to hang some of my comments is that
developed by Martha Nussbaum,[1] in her book, *Women and Human
Development*. She proposes the theory of capabilities. She builds on
Sen's[2] work and speaks to the development of the individual and the
group as social freedoms. She raises the question of convergence and
individuality. "How much in the way of resources is the individual able
to command? What is an individual able to do and to be?" Here she
raises both individual and social responsibility for the development of
human capabilities to their fullest and the issue of social justice within a
given context. She illustrates the centrality of this question by focusing
on women. Nussbaum illustrates how education may not be enough
for many women in the world, as they need their worlds organized to
support those freedoms in social ways. She stresses the importance of
seeing education as needing material supports for the engagement of
individuals to gain some measure of the quality of life they desire and
have reason to value. In other words, freedom is not just an outcome
in the form of the right to free speech, but entails the social conditions

that would permit the exercise of free speech. One without the other does not permit the full expression of a capability of the individual. In Nussbaum's words, "suitable external conditions for the exercise of the function"[3] are necessary.

All that the teachers at PS 165 accomplished would not have been possible if they had not developed their individual capabilities, or if the institutional capabilities had not been available. Concomitant with the spirit of generosity offered by the freedoms was the responsibility for thinking through, planning, and making the linguistic, intellectual and professional freedoms real in everyday life. Thus, these teachers were engaged in development as freedom, the expansion of freedoms for themselves as well as for those around them. As reflective practitioners, they contemplated their lives and the lives of their students. They were responsible for their own past roles in the academic and social development of the children. They reflected on the historical and current despair and injustices they observed in the lives of the students and their community. The teachers named the injustices they saw everyday in the faces of the non-English proficient children they taught as the continuous sabotage of bilingual policies, the lack of materials, and the daily challenges they faced in making language equity a reality. Their hope was to provide their students a linguistic choice and the capability of engaging academically with both English and Spanish. They exercised agency in rethinking their own views, beliefs, and practices about teaching in their desire to provide the English-language learners with an environment in which they could use all the linguistic resources they had available in the two languages that were mediums of instruction so as to acquire not only the legacy of knowledge humanity offered them but also a space of intellectual freedom. As Eugenio Maria de Hostos[4] proposed, the "degree of freedom of an individual or a society is directly related to the manner in which one is educated to think." They were, even more importantly, struggling to provide children with the capability of critical thinking to make choices of what they valued and desired in their future lives, including the role the two languages would play.

The teachers were, ultimately, involved in the project of development as freedom, where they were trying to ensure greater freedoms for children linguistically, intellectually, and socially. In the process, they found the seeds of freedom for themselves as teachers.

What was evident throughout, as Nussbaum proposes, is that the administrative context of support and challenge was critical in providing the material and policy resources for language, teacher, and intellectual development. Ruth was truly an inspirational leader with a moral imperative,[5] but the story was not just about an individual leader. Ruth could cause this transformation to occur or create the conditions necessary, but despite her inspirational qualities, it was also necessary for the other actors, that is, the teachers, to take a stance that would make it happen. Freedom from obstacles and constraint were ensured through policies and practices, and with the support of human and financial resources. The two were intertwined and connected in their desires and actions.

My question is to what extent can the individual freedoms, such as the ones named within, be ensured if the U.S. citizenry is not supporting the suitable external conditions of linguistic freedom in schools? It is a question that ought to be raised at many levels, even in educational settings beyond schools. My decision to tell this story as one of hope was compelled by the many questions it raises. It raises questions about the self (mine and ourselves) and about individual schools and school systems. It also raises, more broadly, the issue of freedom within our society. What do we want to leave as a legacy to our future—our children and theirs?

It also raises the question of replicability. While writing this book, I came across Erin Grunwell[6] and her students' book, *The Freedom Writers Diary*. It made me think hard about the issue. It is also a story of hope and possibilities from individual to classroom to institution to society. The students in Grunwell's classroom, who come from very similar background as the students at PS 165, while at a secondary level and most knowing English, helped me to crystallize this issue of replicability, or scaling, as we often now hear in educational circles. Despite all the encountered restraints in their short lives, Grunwell's young adolescent students were successful by any standard. Grunwell had seen to it by confronting these young adults squarely, while showing caring when they thought they could not continue and by creating as many collective structures as possible to support them. Their accomplishments were so big that Paramount Pictures made a film about them. At the end of the film, the head of the English department raises this important question—she wanted to know about the practicality and replicability of this lone teacher's methods. It is very likely that if you arrived at this page, you may be wondering, like the head of the English department, about the replicability of what was written within. Grunwell, in the film, had a great response, so I will steal it—"I do not know whether it is replicable."

I watched this movie with a friend, whose reaction at the end of the movie had a message that also needs to get out: "We know what works;

we know what research tells us works. It is the system that does not allow it to happen." After thinking about her response, I would say, "Yes, this is true." We need what Nussbaum[7] calls the material support or the "combined conditions." Yet, I want to leave the reader with a series of questions. What if you were to wait for the system to allow this to happen, do you think it would happen? Who would be the cause of nothing occurring? What if you did not wait, like Grunwell or the teachers of PS 165? How would you know what is possible, and how would a different system be created if we, individually and collectively, do not try?

ENDNOTES

1. Nussbaum, Martha C. *Women and Human Development: The Capabilities Approach.* (Cambridge: UK, Cambridge University Press, 2000).

2. Sen, Amartya. *Development as Freedom.* (New York: Random House, 1999).

3. Nussbaum, Martha C. *Women and Human Development*, pp. 84-85.

4. Palmer, Joy A. *Fifty Major Thinkers in Education: From Piaget to the Present Day.* (New York: Routledge Publishers, 2001).

5. Fullan, Michael. *The Moral Imperative of School Leadership.* (Thousand Oaks, CA: Corwin Press, 2003).

6. Grunwell, Erin. *The Freedom Writers Diary.* (New York: Doubleday, 1999). The book was later made into a movie directed by Richard LaGravenes in which Hillary Swank plays the part of Erin. The Freedom Writers created a foundation (www.freedomwritersfoundation.org) that keeps Erin and the students connected to their promise to change education and is dedicated to decreasing high school dropouts, particularly in situations where young people are labeled by the educational system as "unteachable, below average, or delinquent." Currently Erin Grunwell serves as the president of the foundation.

7. Nussbaum, *Women and Human Development.*

INDEX

ABOUT THE AUTHOR

❧

María E. Torres-Guzmán is a Professor of Bilingual/Bicultural Education at Teachers College, Columbia University. Her publications have explored alternative perspectives on the relationship between multiple languages, multiple cultures, and learning. Her current interests focus on linguocultural spaces and personal historical narratives.